Bridging the Pacific

Bridging the Pacific

Searching for Cross-Cultural Understanding Between the United States and China

Shouhua Qi

China Books & Periodicals, Inc.
San Francisco

Copyright © 2000 by Shouhua Qi

All rights reserved under International and
Pan American Copyright Conventions.
Published in the United States by
China Books and Periodicals, Inc.

ISBN 0-8351-2675-7

Library of Congress Cataloging-in-Publication Data

Ch'i, Shou-hua.
   Bridging the Pacific : searching for cross-cultural understanding between the United States and China / Shouhua Qi.-- 1st ed.
   p. cm.
   ISBN 0-8351-2675-7 (pbk.)
   1. United States--Relations--China. 2. China--Relations--United States. 3. East and West. 4. Intercultural communication--United States. 5. Intercultural communication--China. 6. Ch'o', Shou-hua. 7. Chinese Americans--Biography. 8. Immigrants--United States--Biography. I. Title.

E183.8.C5 C43415 2000
303.48'273051--dc21

                                                                           00-023370

Printed in Canada
First Edition

Book and cover design by Linda Revel

China Books & Periodicals, Inc.
2929 Twenty-fourth Street
San Francisco, CA   94110
www.chinabooks.com

Contents

PREFACE	VII
PART I THE SWALLOW	1
The Swallow	3
My Car Complex	13
Great Expectations	35
A Dark-Haired, Yellow-Faced English Professor	49
A Letter in Spring	67
The In-laws Are Coming	73
PART II THE TANGO	91
Sino-American Tango	93
Taiwan Strait Crisis: More Complex Than Morality Play	93
Mutual Engagement Best for U.S. and China	95
Did You Hear a Clash?	98
A Bridge into the 21st Century	101
Leadership	104
Frenzied Fallacies	107
Frailty, Thy Name is. . .	111
Dance with Chains	115
Deng's Epic	115
Encouraging Signs	118
Hong Kong at Sunrise	121
China's Gamble	124
The Albatross over the Square	128
China at Crossroads	131

Random Notes	135
I Want a Bride	135
A Visit to Hope's Home	137
I Broke My Promise	140
"Where Can We Go Find Jobs, Sir?"	142
Father Touched My Forehead	143
Have You Made Fortune Lately?	145
PART III A HAPPY MEAN?	147
Blues, Fervor, and Stupidity	149
Election Year Blues on the Sidelines	149
Olympic Fervor Felt First-Hand in China	153
It's the Names, Stupid!	156
Tiger! Tiger!	159
What's Up? Presidential Sex Scandals, The Law of the Smelly Bean Curd and Other Trivia	163
Forever Behind: Confessions of a Half-Hearted Hardy Fan	177
Why Do These Flowers Blooming Inside the Garden Wall Smell More Fragrant to Passersby Outside?	185
Hubris and Humility: Is There a Happy Mean?	199

Preface

IT WAS EARLY 1996. The skies over the Taiwan Strait were clouded with smoke from a recent, live missile exercise. Huge, stoic shadows of aircraft carriers loomed just miles away from the southern mouth of the strait that had been sealed off for war games. The specter of another major, bloody showdown hung in the air.

As a Chinese scholar living and teaching in the U.S., I felt called upon to help build a bridge of understanding across the muddy waters of the Pacific so that there would be peace not only "in our time," but also in the 21st century between two of the most important countries in the world. This self-assigned (and exaggerated, perhaps) mission resulted in many guest columns and essays on U.S.-China relations and on cross-cultural (mis)understanding, published in various newspapers and magazines. These and other published writings, with only a few minor stylistic changes, are now collected in this book titled *Bridging The Pacific: The Search for Cross-Cultural Understanding Between the United States and China*.

Also collected in this book are a few conference papers (e.g., "Forever Behind," "Why Do These Flowers. . .") on pertinent topics, a few personal essays and other writings, penned more recently and specifically for this book (e.g., "My Car Complex," "Great Expectations," "A Dark-Haired, Yellow-Faced English Professor," "The In-laws are Coming," "What's Up," "Random Notes"), a short story ("The Swallow," which is based on my real-life experience and has been published before both in Chinese and in English). A Chinese version of "A Letter in Spring" was published in China in 1996.

The writings are organized into three groups according to their thematic similarities (inevitably, with some overlapping):

Those in "Part I: The Swallow" are of a more personal nature; those in "Part II: The Tango" are concerned more with Sino-American relations and recent development in China; and those in "Part III: A Happy Mean?" focus more on cross-cultural (mis)understanding. Original dates of publication are given for many of the writings so that they can be read in their proper historical contexts.

Is an ocean as wide as the Pacific bridgeable? Can we find a happy mean between old and new, East and West, friend and foe? As I write this preface on a particularly beautiful, sunny Pennsylvania afternoon in late August 1999, the skies over the Taiwan Strait, and across the Pacific, for that matter, are again being visited by the same specter in a manner as surreal and depressing as three years ago. The political wisdom I was calling for then seems to remain either nonexistent or as elusive as ever. However, there is still hope and there is no reason to give up despite setbacks of Sisyphean proportions.

I'd like to thank Dr. William Morgan, professor of English at Illinois State University and a good friend of mine, who first put the idea of assembling a collection like this into my head.

My special thanks go to many of my friends and colleagues in Harrisburg, PA and across the country who have pumped more confidence into me by telling me that they enjoyed reading my writings—despite the fact that they might disagree with me passionately. I'm also grateful to the editors of various publications for giving me permission to reprint many of the op-ed pieces and other writings in this book.

To Mr. Greg Jones of China Books, I owe so much for the enthusiastic response when I first approached him with a tentative idea for this collection, and for the unfaltering support he has given me ever since. To Mr. Baolin Ma of the same press, I also owe a lot for his warm support and for helping me publish a Chinese edition of this book in China. To my editor, Mr. Erik Noyes, a writer himself and a fellow believer in tough love, for combing through the manuscript with his sharp and honest eye and for his numerous insightful comments and invaluable suggestions.

Finally, I want to thank my wife, Xiaohong, and my son, Frank. They are forever my first (and most critical, for that matter) readers, and my loyal and most zealous cheerleaders. They have had to put up with my erratic schedule and occasional (they both flatly reject this epithet as gross understatement) "eccentric outbursts" with love, patience, and good humor.

*For My Wife Xiaohong
and My Son Frank —*

Part I
The Swallow

The Swallow

A BULKY BLUE canvas bag in each hand, and a bulging greenish nylon handbag vised precariously under my right arm, I struggled out of the sliding door of Terminal 1 at O'Hare International Airport. The handbag strap was already broken, a little inconvenience that had happened at the crowded Shanghai International Airport over 20 hours earlier. Every single joint from my shoulders down to my fingertips was being stretched to its utmost limits. My 5' 5" stature shrank a couple of inches under the burden.

The gusty, freezing waves of Lake Michigan wind caught me as I exited the terminal. The warm moisture on the thick lenses above my nose instantly froze into something resembling the fine sugar coating on a Dunkin' Donut.

A huge shadow penetrated the fog.

"L'me len' cha a 'and?" offered the shadow in a deep, throaty voice. Before I could respond, my left hand felt a yank, and a sudden loss of weight. I became unbalanced, teetering uncontrollably in a rightward orientation. Switching the handbag to my now freed left hand to regain balance, I labored after the bearish outline across the busy driveway toward what seemed a bus stop sign on the narrow pedestrian island.

"Thank you very much!" I gasped when I had finally caught up with my as-yet-unintroduced new friend, each syllable bouncing off my almost frozen mouth into the cold air like a fugitive being hunted down by a tail of overly zealous hot steam. I removed my glasses and wiped them roughly with the handkerchief that had been abused a thousand times to dry the torrential sweat from my forehead. In the now somewhat-less-foggy view, a pair of big, shining eyes appeared. In those eyes, black was purely black and white was purely white. They stared down at me hungrily.

I was aware of the need to express my gratitude more than verbally. I dug frantically in the nylon handbag for my wallet. Then, I stopped in the wake of a sudden realization. Cold sweat graced my forehead again.

"Don't y' wanna tip?" my new friend urged, noticing my hesitation. I mumbled an apology. Throwing me a dirty look, the erstwhile friend hurried away to help other passengers who were currently being spit out of the sliding door.

Multi-lanes. Overpasses. Cars. Yellow Cabs. Limos. Buses. Shuttles. White snow. Muddy snow. Hazy street lights.

Where is my Swallow? The spring dream and sweet melody dancing in and out of my country house?

No borrowing of your charcoal,
no borrowing of your rice,
only borrowing your house to give birth to our babies.

My father used to tell me that this was what the swallows were singing to us every springtime when they returned, asking for permission to build their new nests in the roof beams of our house.

I had become infatuated with the name of the shuttle bus service the first time I saw it in the schedule book sent by my thoughtful foreign student advisor. I'd rolled it over on my tongue a hundred times and every time, I savored the same sweet, childhood memories.

Five minutes passed. Ten minutes passed. Buses came and went. No Swallows. The back of my shirt was frozen stiff with what had once been sweat. My nose, mouth and hands were approaching numbness.

Then, I saw a bus, with the well-known name on its forehead. It pulled up gracefully. My heart beat wildly as it had on a certain spring afternoon nine years before when I saw a beautiful girl, now my wife, walking towards me along a little path of the Xuan Wu Lake right across from the new railway station. We were going out on a first date.

The spring dream. The sweet melody—

A stout guy in a short-sleeved uniform interrupted my reveries as he dismounted the big bird energetically. He looked strong and warm, oblivious to the below zero temperature. While he was opening up the luggage trunk, I hastened over.

"Are you going to Bloomington-Normal, Sir?" my mouth, now frozen out of shape, managed. My whole body shivered.

The Swallow

The cold, however, was quickly succumbing to a sickening urge to visit a restroom.

"Yep!" Short as the answer was, it had to be squeezed out through a piece of pinkish gum that had been twisted and chewed God knows how many times between crushing teeth. I hastened back, dragging the two heavy bags closer to the Swallow. As I turned them over to the warm-looking driver, I sighed. I felt a great sense of relief and accomplishment.

As I was mounting the bird, my glasses were once again overcome by a fog. This time, the moisture was due to the waves of heat coming from inside the bus. After wiping off the moisture with my trusty handkerchief, I bent down to fumble inside the handbag with its broken strap. I succeeded in digging out all of my money: a $100 bill. It was hidden in the bundle comprised of my passport, the IAP 66 form, my admission notice and letters from the foreign student advisor and director of graduate studies.

This bundle was further buried deep in rubber-soled cloth shoes, homemade diapers, tiny, cute, and fluffy baby clothes, sent by a mother for her daughter who was due at any time. The mother was a friend of my in-laws and the daughter's husband was a doctoral student at Champaign-Urbana.

The admission notice would entitle me to a $10 discount for this ride. So the total cost would come down to $20. Not bad, considering the 130 miles distance—and, of course, the snow.

I handed the $100 bill to the driver with the admission notice. His chewing muscles were still wriggling methodically in his warm and ruddy cheeks.

"What's de's?" the driver exclaimed, spitting whatever was left of the tasteless gum into something next to his seat. He gave a swift, backward glance at the whole bus. "Think I'm some kinda Donald Trump walkin' 'round w' bundles o' bills, eh!" He thrust the currency and the admission notice back to me. His face glowered with indignation, giving it an even healthier look.

I was dumbfounded. However naive I am, I have never bought into the myth of gold-paved streets in America, but a $100 bill? I turned to the passengers in the bus. Some were already dozing off into their own, unknown dreamlands, others stared ahead, blankly.

Suddenly, I saw another face: the expressionless face of a pretty girl sitting behind the glass window of a branch office of the Central Bank in downtown Nanjing, my hometown. I had taken the afternoon off and biked all the way to that office to prevent this very scenario from taking place. There were several windows. I couldn't be sure now whether I had made my choice because the line there was shorter or because the teller was younger and prettier. At any rate, after waiting in the line for quite some time, I approached her majestic-looking window and asked this young, pretty teller to change the $100 bill.

I had obtained the $100 bill through an earlier, clandestine exchange with David in a dimly-lit back room of a small family restaurant. David, son of a mayor of a small town in California, was then studying at Nanjing University. He and his buddies liked to frequent such restaurants to satisfy their taste for Hot 'n Sour Tofu, Princess Chicken and other exotic dishes. Occasionally, they would slip into the back rooms to gratify other desires of theirs: higher exchange rate for their American dollars. Having become savvy about how things were done locally, they found it difficult to resist the temptation of a vibrant black market which beckoned them with an exchange rate typically three times higher than that offered by the State-run Central Bank. For me, however, it was the most thrilling and illicit adventure I had ever taken. It was as if I had gone behind my wife's back to see a woman of questionable reputation.

"No," the pretty bank teller said in a flat voice, throwing the bill back to me through the tiny hole in her teller window.

"Listen. Please would you change this bill?" The veneer of pride, that came from being a lecturer of English at a prestigious university, began to peel off. "I need the smaller bills. I'm traveling abroad, and I'm sure it will be. . . um. . . inconvenient to. . ."

"How can I tell if that bill of yours is real?" She cut me off, raising her voice to a higher pitch. A flash of emotion flitted across her pretty face.

"Well, you have a well-trained eye. I'm sure that if it was counterfeit, you would be able to tell right away." I held on, unwilling to give up my only hope.

"Nuisance!" she cut me short, again, utterly losing her patience. Her face had more color now, making it even more lovely. "Next!" she shouted to the person behind me, who eagerly elbowed me to the side.

That was the last straw. All the humiliations I had had to

The Swallow

put up with so far during the last few months of my efforts to overcome each of the numerous obstacles, from known and unknown directions, had come to a head and finally found their target for retaliation.

The worst of these humiliations had been at the hands of university officials. When I went to the University's Office of International Affairs to get its seal on my application for permission to study abroad, the division Party chief-turned-director was sitting behind his big desk, busy signing forms. Having heard the purpose of my visit, he began to lecture me, without raising his rather fleshy face: "All you young teachers care about is going abroad, fooling around for a few years, then dragging back home a few foreign made TV sets, fridges, washer-dryers, microwaves. . . For what? To show off! I've got you all figured out. No sour grapes from yours truly here, 'cause who hasn't seen them foreign things. . . "

I nearly choked. Speechless. I had never met this guy before, and I felt his sermon was totally uncalled for. I quickly let my emotions get the better of me, and rose up in my own defense. A few minutes later, I stormed out of his office, feeling rather good about myself, but empty-handed.

Then, there was the University's head accountant who moaned and groaned through his nose after practically making me beg for the quota of foreign currency, i.e., U. S. dollars, I was entitled to exchange per university policies. I needed the money to buy the ticket for my flight.

After taking several deep drags at his cigarette which had burned almost to the butt, he offered me the black market rate, with apparent reluctance in his voice. I was told later that the results might have been more encouraging if I had approached both of these university officials differently, e.g., with cartons of Kent, 555, Marlboro, etc.

And now, here was the unfortunate who would pay for all the indignities. I would have spit all over her with the most obscene words on earth, but being brought up by strict parents, I hadn't ever truly mastered that art in my native tongue. I had a whole heart to ditch the Confucian "Gentleman uses his mouth rather than his fists" code and smash that cute little nose in her lovely face. Alas, my arm was not long enough, and the thick window glass was intimidating and seemingly impenetrable enough to discourage these thoughts.

All the literary prowess I had imagined to be in possession

of—critiques published in academic journals, books translated, near perfect TOEFL score, impressive GRE percentile, all of the things that had earned me the graduate school admission and teaching assistantship—all of this proved useless to me now. As I was turning away, foaming with anger, an English expression suddenly jumped to the tip of my tongue. "Damn you!" I fired. That would do the job here.

I missed the target miserably. Her pretty face was still intact with no smoking holes or crushed bone from the verbal gunshot. Apparently, her ignorance of the lethality of that outburst was her best armor. Nevertheless, I experienced the same sensation that Ah Q—the twisted protagonist in the famous Lu Xun novella—got from touching the smooth, hairless top of a young nun's head. I felt a deep, yet fleeting, satisfaction that comes from exacting revenge.

"Next!" the now-gumless driver of the Swallow Shuttle bellowed.

"What should I do, sir?" I woke up from the reverie and moved to the side to let others pay their fare. Maybe I should use that same lethal weapon to take care of the predicament here. . . No, I didn't have the guts to pull the trigger.

"L'cha know later, okay?" the driver was more than annoyed now. Somehow I had become the object of his utter irritation. Had he placed the blame on me for the tastelessness of his treasured gum also?

The bus began to move. Staring outside from my seat, I could have sworn I saw a recognizable, pretty face, sneering at me from behind the thick glass window. Damn.

When the bus stopped at another terminal, the driver turned to me. "See de guy in a re' hat o'er d're? Hurry it up!"

I huffed it towards the aforementioned red-hatted, Santa-looking fellow. He sat perched inside a glass structure near a sliding door. In his hand, he held an enormous money-holder. Before I could make any explanation, my savior took the $100 bill and gave me some $20's, $10's, and $5's. I hurried back to the Swallow, pulled out one $20 bill, and handed it over to the driver. Success! I felt like saying, "Take that, Gum-chewer!" But once again, I refrained.

The bus finally pulled away from the airport terminals now. First Interstate 295, then to Interstate 55. Flat, snow-covered land stretched into the endless unknown and eventually merged with the misty, somber sky.

More than 15 hours of flying over the Pacific. Another 4

The Swallow 9

hours over North America. Across a dozen time zones. Ten thousand miles away from home. Mei Guo, the Beautiful Country, remained as bewildering in direct contact as in the book I once co-translated: *America through a Kaleidoscope*. Why was I coming to America? I wondered. To borrow charcoal? Rice? To look for gold? To satisfy the expectations I had felt in the eyes of my wife and family? To keep my place as one of the most promising young scholars in the foreign languages department? To pacify something in me which had hitherto been dormant, but had suddenly become restless? Or was it to answer a calling I had heard only vaguely? I couldn't tell, and I didn't want to be bothered by these questions now.

The Swallow sailed gleefully down the interstate. Perhaps my overactive imagination was getting the better of me, but the bus seemed to flit and dance onto and off of the highway to drop off old passengers and pick up new ones at small towns. All of the passengers would be plunged into freezing cold when the door opened. We would finally recover long after the door was shut.

After about 2 and a half hours, the Swallow made a stop in front of a fast food restaurant in Pontiac, a small town 35 miles north of Bloomington-Normal.

"Y' folks can get off 'n' use de restroom." The shirt-sleeved driver sounded warm and thoughtful. I noticed that he had set to work on another piece of gum with obvious relish.

Feeling the bursting pressure in my bladder, I eagerly followed the single file line off the bus.

There were more than half a dozen guys crowded into the small single-toilet restroom of the fast food restaurant. Every one of them seemed to be taking his time deliberately, thoroughly enjoying the long-awaited act of relief. The air grew more and more repugnant. Of course, I was the last one out of the restroom.

My heart skipped a beat. Where is my Swallow? I rushed to the spot where the bus had been. It wasn't there. I rushed to the back of the restaurant, staggering over a thickly glaciated little path. All I saw were icicles, hanging from the eaves. I rushed to the Clark gas station next to the restaurant. A middle-aged, balding employee there told me that the bus had just taken off ten seconds before.

Everything I had was on that bus: the two heavy bags in the luggage compartment, the bulging handbag underneath the seat, the $80 in small bills, my personal documents, the homemade shoes, diapers and fluffy baby clothes. Everything was on that bus, everything but me.

"What do I do? What should I do?" I asked in a panicky voice, half to myself and half to the gas station employee. I felt a sickening urge to use the restroom, though I had just been there. The cold winds from across Lake Michigan were mercilessly whipping at me now.

The balding employee was sympathetic. He dug into his pockets, produced a handful of quarters, dimes and nickels, and pushed them to me across the glass countertop. "Try th' payphone ou' there 'n' probably..."

As one being sucked into a freezing whirlpool while clutching at a straw, I grabbed the coins and hurried to the phone. It stood right next to a "NO EXIT" sign, near the station entrance.

No matter how hard I ransacked my memory, I couldn't turn up any numbers. The massive, worn-out phone book dangling from the booth looked too intimidating to even attempt to decipher. I began to study the instructions on the cover of the phone. Then, my trembling fingers picked up the handset and dialed "0."

A sweet voice answered at the other end. "This is Rachel at GTE North. Can I help you?" She sounded so far away, and so meltingly warm. I saw myself toddling towards the voice and nestling my head into its soft chest shamelessly.

I stumbled through an awkward explanation. Rachel told me to calm down and hold on. She dialed some numbers. Somebody picked up after 4 or 5 rings.

"Hi! Is this the Swallow Shuttle Station?" I heard Rachel asking.

"uh-huh," a male voice answered.

"This is Rachel from GTE North. I'd like to talk to your manager."

"Speaking."

"It's like this. One of your buses from Chicago has just left behind a passenger at Pontiac."

"Really? That's too bad. But can't do nothin' about i'." Swallow Shuttle sounded not so warm. I felt the freezing whirlpool sucking me downward again.

"Well, could you hold and I'll let my supervisor talk to you?" Rachel's voice was as composed as before.

After a prolonged moment of quiet where all I could hear

The Swallow

was the subtle static of intervening miles, I heard another female voice. It was richer and more authoritative.

"Hi, this is Nancy Kostenkowaski, supervisor at GTE North. Could you tell me who I am talking to?"

"Bill McKinley," Bill faltered.

"Mr. McKinley, you know what's happened to one of your passengers, right?"

"Yes."

"And yet, you don't intend to do anything about it?"

"Don't expect me to ask th' bus to turn around, with all th' other passengers on board, do ya?"

"Your Shuttle has full responsibility for each of its passengers. Perhaps you don't realize the consequences of having left behind a passenger?"

"Sure do, but. . ."

"I hate to step out of my bounds, but if you don't do something to take care of this, I promise you I won't mind going all the way to your superior. . . "

"Well," Bill hesitated, "uh, how about th' guy wai' for our 11:30 bus?"

"That's 3 hours from now!" Nancy was exasperated.

"See. . ."

"All right," Nancy cut him short, "you could at least contact that bus of yours and make sure nothing is lost."

"Okey-dokey."

Bill addressed me with a few questions about the bags. I was at a loss for a moment. I had been so engrossed in the exchanges between the operators of GTE North and the Swallow manager that I had forgotten what was at stake for myself. After obtaining all the necessary descriptions and telling me where to pick up the baggage the next morning, Bill hung up.

"Well, we still have this problem of how to get you to Illinois State, right?" Nancy addressed me. "Let me see," she began to think. I could see a few deep lines forming between the most beautiful eyebrows I had never seen. "Okay, how about giving me the name of your foreign student advisor?" I gave it to her, and she dialed.

The phone rang, somewhere in the distance. A voice identified herself as the foreign student advisor. She was very concerned. There was a short pause. Then, she said that she and her husband, a senior professor of history, were on their way.

After thanking Rachel and Nancy, I hung up. The mist had begun to dissolve. Miraculously, the night sky was clearing up, and turning deep blue. I thought I heard wild geese chanting rhythmically somewhere high in the sky. What are they singing? I wondered. The same song the swallows in my childhood memories were singing every spring? And where are they going? This was early January, 1989, an extremely cold winter. Spring was still far, far away. Totally exhausted, I took a deep breath and trudged back to the well-lit gas station. "Tomorrow," I mumbled to myself.

My Car Complex

I

FIRST, THE SOUND: a low-keyed humming sound, cutting through the air. It approached, grew closer and louder. Abruptly, it stopped. Doors opened, and our distinguished guests stood before us. We broke into a warm applause, cheering: "Welcome! Welcome!" We—pupils and teachers of a rural elementary school of Nanjing—had been waiting at the school's gate excitedly. We were told that our guests were from Albania: the lone, shining beacon of Socialism on the otherwise dark continent of Europe.

I was a second-grader then. Chosen by my school, together with a few other boys and girls, to perform before our distinguished guests. Besides being excited, I had something else on my mind: I was worried about my shoes. The heels were very worn and when I ran or danced, they would fall off. Indeed, I could even see the big toe of my right foot sneaking out of the shoe. My teacher told me not to worry. I could run and dance barefooted, and our guests would not mind. They were friends, and friends would never pass shoe-based judgement.

After their brief stay, our guests departed. Once again, there was the humming sound. The wheels kicked up dust on the dirt country road. The humming gradually got smaller and smaller until it was perceptible only as an absence.

What kind of cars had our distinguished guests arrived in on that particular day? Was it the Russian made, beetle-shaped Volga? What was the color? Gray? Black? Light Blue? I couldn't recall, not even on a comfortable couch under hypnosis. But that first impression of a *xiaoqiche,* sedan car, is forever associated with something mysterious, respectable, and authoritative. Its considerable ethos burned deep in my young memory.

That was in the mid 1960s. At that time, and for many years to come, my family's main means of transportation was my father's bicycle. The principal of a middle school, he was one of the few people in an area of several square miles who actually had a bicycle. I was privileged, too, often riding either in the front or on the back of dad's bike, a *yongjiu,* "Everlasting" model made in Shanghai.

Sitting in the front seat—nothing but the thin horizontal bar—I would gaze at the wheel immediately below me, revolving and revolving on the country road. I would watch, mesmerized, until I grew dizzy and felt my head was revolving with the wheel.

I'd chase the butterflies and dragonflies with my eyes as they flitted and flew around us playfully. Oh, there were so many butterflies, and they were of so many different colors: white, yellow, pink, and freckled. Dragonflies dove all around us and pulled up close in the blink of an eye like tiny fighter jets.

One evening, when I was riding in the back seat, my right foot got caught in the rear wheel; my dad heard a cracking noise as the bike jolted to a halt. Dad carried me to a house nearby, checking to see if any bone was broken. I had been lucky. The family applied some cooking oil to my foot, and we went on our way home. My right foot remained swollen like a big melon for days, and I was house bound. I was not crippled by the mishap, though.

That *yongjiu* bike caused us some trouble, too. One day at the beginning of the "Great Proletarian Cultural Revolution," a regiment of Red Guards had come to confiscate the bike. They cited it as evidence of my father's life as a "capitalist-roader." Only my brother and I were at home when they arrived.

Our good neighbors, having got wind of the approaching Red Guards, took it upon themselves to protect us and hide the bike in one of their homes. Disappointed, the Red Guards kicked around, cussed profusely, and left.

More than ten years later, that same bike was to carry my own family—my wife sitting in the back and my son sitting in the front—to market, to parks and to visit friends and family. Rain or shine, for six years, I chauffeured my son between the kindergarten and our home, until the end of 1988. It was tough in the winter when a stiff wind would blow right in his face.

Of course, there were the public buses, but they were notorious for being crowded and perpetually delayed. I remember

My Car Complex 15

when my son was still a baby, I would carry him in my arms and try to squeeze onto buses back-first so that he would not get hurt.

Despite our dependence on the public transportation, the bike, and Bus No. 11—11 standing for a pair of legs—I had ridden in a *xiaoqiche* before coming to the States. After graduating from college, I married a beautiful girl whose father—a veteran who had "joined the revolution" close to the end of WWII—belonged to a privileged class in China who enjoyed the luxury of riding in State-provided cars. While it is not a big deal today, it was quite a mark of one's social status back in the 80s and earlier.

As a son-in-law, I benefited now and then from an extended version of that privilege. Every time I rode in the car, I had mixed feelings. Looking through the window, I saw folks fighting to get on crowded buses, bikes streaming down bustling streets and peasants trudging under their heavy loads of vegetables. I can still see their big baskets, piled high for market. I can see the bamboo carrying poles on their shoulders, bending, straining under the weight. I felt somewhat superior to these people, but more than anything, I felt guilty. I didn't deserve this privilege. I hadn't earned it. My parents, my brother and sister, my friends and all those people and peasants on the streets were entitled to no less than I was.

The day before my departure to the States, my parents had thrown a farewell party. My wife's brother came in a Beijing jeep. I knew this was a rare chance. I knew somehow that one day I'd have my own car and I needed to learn to drive.

I asked, and my brother-in-law brought me and the jeep to my father's middle school. He showed me where the gas and brake pedals were and how to turn the ignition key. I got into the driver's seat, turned the key nervously, and drove around the 400-meter track a few times.

I had drunk a few glasses of *yanghe*—a popular brand of strong liquor in my home province Jiangsu—but my mind was clear. I was excited. Another brother-in-law of mine—my sister's husband—who had come along, wanted to take it for a spin, too. He assured the other brother-in-law that he had previous driving experience. Perhaps his skills had gotten rusty at that time, or he had had a drop too much to drink. At any rate, he tramped the gas and the jeep sprang forward like an angry horse. It left the track quickly and rammed head-on into the solid trunk of a big tree. The result was a V-shaped front bumper. In that way, my first car-driving adventure came to an abrupt end.

The next day, my father-in-law arranged for a car to take me and my things to the train station. From there I'd go to Shanghai and then board a plane to the United States. Everybody else was to take the buses. I looked at my father and mother who were coming to see me off. No, for once at least, I wanted them to ride in the car and I'd take the bus instead. They would not hear of it. I almost lost my temper trying to get them into the car, and they finally agreed.

As I rode the crowded bus to the train station, I felt something warm dripping down my cheeks. I tried without success to hold it back.

II

WHEN I GOT OFF the Boeing 747 at Chicago's O'Hare International Airport early that January in 1989, I had only one $100 bill in my wallet. New and practically worthless in an unknown country, I had so many things to worry about that buying a car was the last thing on my mind.

Somehow, I settled down in my new home: the basement of a two-story house, owned by a single mother in her late 20s, on a street within walking distance of the university. My roommate situation was interesting. I roomed with a visiting scholar from Liaoning province whose specialty was fuzzy mathematics, and a graduate student from Shanghai who was working on his doctoral degree in history. All three of us were new, far from rich and firmly entrenched in the car-less class. While being car-less was not a major hindrance back in China—it only meant that you had to ride public buses or your bike—it could be a real problem in the States where public transportation is largely inadequate, and bicycle riding is a risky means of travel.

In the first few days, we relied on the generosity of our compatriots, other Chinese students who had been in this country longer, and who now had the enviable luxury of driving around in their own cars. Of these, Lao Liu and Xiao Fang were the most helpful.

My Car Complex

On our first grocery shopping trip, I bought some salt, soy source, white bread, rice, and the cheapest vegetables—potatoes and cabbages—and the cheapest meat—chicken leg quarters at $.30 a pound. With these supplies in place, I could now cook and eat. That was the day I felt that my life in this new country had officially begun.

When our supplies ran low, which never took long, we encountered real problems. Should we call our Chinese friends to take us grocery shopping again? Everybody was always very busy, and we knew our constant reliance would quickly become an annoyance. We didn't have phone service in our basement anyway. In fact, we didn't have TV, radio, or even a newspaper. After weighing our options, we decided to make use of our legs and walk to the nearest grocery store.

Walking to the grocery store should have meant nothing to me. When I was receiving "re-education" from the peasants in the mid 70s, I, together with a couple of young friends, had pulled a heavily loaded *banche*—a two-wheeled cart—everyday for a whole summer, covering 15 to 20 miles each way. The cart was so heavy that we had to bend our backs nearly parallel with the ground in order to kick the ground firmly enough to make the wheels move. I had also worked in a plant manufacturing construction material such as bricks and shingles. The centuries old way of making these products was to burn the sun-dried mud adobe bricks and shingles in a big cave-like kiln. When they were ready for unloading, the inside of the kiln was still at least 150° Celsius. With a big fan blowing into the kiln, I'd go in, grab the bricks or shingles with my hands, place them on that two-wheeled cart, and pull them all the way to market.

Walking to the grocery store in the U.S. was more hazardous. The road leading to the grocery store, which was about four miles away, did not have any sidewalks. While a gallon of milk, a five-pound bag of potatoes and a head of cabbage are not really heavy, the distance made these aggregate items feel, quite literally, like a ton of bricks. To make it worse, with cars racing by at 40 or 50 miles an hour, I felt as if we were crawling at a snail's pace. The only thing that helped was the company: we talked and talked while tramping along on that endless road.

When we got back to our home in the basement, it was already dark. I dropped the load on the floor right away, and felt the ache settle into my arms and shoulders. We sat there for a few minutes, catching our breath.

As it so happened, it was Friday. The single mother landlady had her stereo blaring. I didn't know if it was rock 'n roll or heavy metal, but the music was thunderous. It sounded as if someone was angrily beating the hell out of the drums. We also listened to the pounding of her kids' feet as they chased each other. Their tiny feet attacked the floor like drumsticks. The floor must have been paper thin. Maybe there were small cracks. At any rate, it was far from soundproof. So we sat there as the sky exploded right over our heads.

The weekend mood was contagious, though. Soon, we began to sing one song after another: all the songs we knew or could think of, folksy or revolutionary, Peking Opera, or a local melody. Some of the lyrics were shamelessly political. They sent goose bumps down my spine. We sang until we couldn't sing any more. Eventually, the thunderstorm blew itself out. Then, we remembered our hunger and started to cook to appease our stomachs.

Sometimes, our young landlady's boyfriend would come and visit. When they had eaten and drunk their fill, the night became quiet. Then, the ritual would begin and titillating noise would find its way down through the thin floor: first the giggling, telling each other to stop it, then heavy breathing, and the sky over the basement shaking rhythmically, finally more giggling and water splashing in the shower. The world above us would rise to a dizzying crescendo before coming to a halt completely, leaving three hot-blooded men in the basement below. Nothing—no grand theorem in fuzzy mathematics, no winds of war in history, no Chomsky, Shakespeare or Hardy— could compare to the intensity of life that was unfolding in the almost weekly drama above us. Is it clear that concentration on books was a bit hard to achieve?

Car-less, we would make journeys on foot to the grocery store every five or ten days. At least during this time of comparative austerity, my bank account was becoming bigger, however slow that growth was. I had a full teaching assistantship, the rent for my little room in the basement was manageable, and I was working in the student cafeteria. My top priority then was to save enough to reimburse a friend of mine who had bought my plane ticket from Shanghai to Chicago. Secondly, I intended to sponsor my wife and son to come and join me. I wasn't ready to buy a car yet.

My Car Complex

While working in one of the student cafeterias, I got to know one of the cooks there. Judy was a middle aged woman, somewhat on the heavy side, but very warm and affable. She liked to chat with the fuzzy math visiting scholar and me. Once she found out about our transportation predicament, she offered to help. She took us to grocery stores in her almost brand new car quite a few times. This was a very cold winter and it snowed often. So her help meant a lot to us.

Other cooks, mostly women, could not appreciate what was going on between Judy and her two Chinese friends. One day, while judy and I were washing broccoli and cutting carrots, and engaged in one of our conversations, one matronly cook walked past us and said, jokingly, "Since you two seem to have so much to talk about, why don't you try dating?"

"I don't see why we can't do that, right?" Judy responded, smilingly. I looked up and saw warmth, expectation, and coyness in her big, sparkling eyes. I smiled, too, but didn't know what to say. In my mind, however, I began to imagine things vaguely: what if she really meant it? I began to stay away from Judy. Did I misunderstand Judy? Did I take a joke too seriously? Or was she really sending me a signal? Was she hurt by my staying away?

Soon, the history student from Shanghai bought an old bicycle. It was very different from the kind of bike in China. It was not designed for carrying things. He rode that bike to the grocery store a couple of times. When he came back, with heavy things dangling on the handle bars, I could see that his trip could not have been a smooth one. He fell off the bike once and seriously hurt one of his wrists. Then, the bike was stolen while chained to a tree, and that was the end of it.

We did have a chance to go to Chicago by car, though. Lao Wang, a visiting scholar from an aerospace program in Beijing, bought a Toyota for about $200. Its sun-bleached interior was pitiful. It must have sat in its original owner's backyard for years before Lao Wang purchased it. The seat covers were so worn that little bundles of sponge and cotton poked through.

The body was in even worse shape: the edges all around the bottom were like borders on a poorly drawn map; they were rusted through with patches missing here and there. It was as if they had been bitten off by a pack of ravenous wolves.

Luckily for the poor car, Lao Wang was a handy man. He got some tools—saws, scissors, screwdrivers, chisels, sheets of thin metal, sandpaper, paint, etc.—and set about resurrecting the car, at least cosmetically. A few weeks later, rather to my surprise, the Toyota looked unrecognizably new. Pleased with his own work, Lao Wang invited us to get into the car and go on an expedition to Chicago, a full 130 miles away.

We were more than eager. The small Toyota could run at a decent speed, carrying the four of us in its somewhat cramped interior. All the way to Chicago, it shook as violently as a malaria patient. The steering wheel, while quivering, showed a stubborn tendency to turn to the left. Lao Wang had to hold it tight with both of his strong arms until his arms quivered in time with the metallic malaria patient.

We lived particularly tense moments whenever a big 18-wheeler roared by. It seemed that any second, if Lao Wang relaxed his firm grip just a little bit, our car would spin off and be sucked under the roaring monster. Death, in the form of a twisted metal tumbleweed seemed imminent at all times, but we were not very concerned, then. The trip itself was exciting enough to make us forget our fears.

We got to Chicago's Chinatown in one piece. While there, we bought a few things: various pickled Chinese vegetables, rice, cooking oil, soy sauce, ginger and other things we normally wouldn't be able to buy from grocery stores in our college town. At the end of the day, Lao Wang was able to drop us off at our basement home, safe and sound and still excited. Looking back on it, it was a hell of a ride and I wouldn't take it again even if somebody were to point a gun at my head, or threaten me with "re-education.".

The following summer, Lao Wang cleaned up his car and drove it hundreds of miles through mountains and hills, passing through Indiana, Ohio, Pennsylvania, and New Jersey to finally arrive in the place to be: New York City. Once there, he applied for a job with a taxi service company, was hired, and began to work there as a cabby.

His car was a two-door thing, small, shabby, still prone to fits of malaria-like shaking, and absolutely without air conditioning. I could not help but chuckle when I tried to imagine in my mind how proud New Yorkers or its equally proud visitors, bulging with flashy shopping bags and boxes in hand, would bend their backs and crawl into the cramped seats in the back of Lao Wang's Toyota. How could they stoop so low? How could they tolerate this? How could they manage? When Lao Wang

My Car Complex

returned, close to the end the summer, I shared this altruistic concern of mine with him. He laughed. He told me—as I was to later find out for myself—that not everyone in Manhattan could afford to ride in limousines. Many would have to make do with his less than comfortable travel arrangement.

Some of his customers, he grinned while adding, did complain profusely about having to bend their backs, about the cramped space, and the steaming heat inside the car, and of course, the constant quivering. There were a few times when his passengers complained so much throughout the ride and had gotten their emotions so worked up that by the time they got out, they would walk off—with their heads high—without bothering to pay the fare. Not to mention forgetting the tip.

Whatever the quality of his services, Lao Wang came back a much richer man. He would spend much less time looking at the prices when we went grocery shopping together. He would simply pick up what he needed and put it in his cart. A few years later, after he graduated with a degree in economics, he went back to Manhattan, found a job with an investment firm and began to play currency exchanges on the Wall Street.

Well before that first spring semester was over, I had begun to look for money-making opportunities, too. Everyday, I would go to the library and check the Classified bulletin board. I would carefully read through all the job ads, studying their detailed descriptions, and pick out only those that I judged myself somewhat qualified for: cook's assistant, dishwasher, cashier, bus boy—you name it.

Then, I'd do some arithmetic on a sheet of paper: pay rate times hours times weeks times months if I were employed by such and such employer. I'd know well in advance how much richer I would be by the end of the summer and what I could do with the money. But, without a car, I couldn't even go and get their application forms. So, the denouement of such dramatic games would always be the same: I would toss my dreams, sketched out on the sheets of paper, into the waste basket.

Seized with sheer desperation a few days before summer break arrived, I bought a round-trip ticket to Boston to visit an American couple, Karen and Mark Bell, whom I had gotten to know through a mutual friend. They had taught in China and had offered to help me locate money-making opportunities.

I stayed at their home for a few days, reading their books,

including their collection of books on China. Among these books was *Two Years in the Melting Pot* by a Chinese journalist from Beijing. Notwithstanding their hospitality, I quickly grew restless.

Mark drove me to Cape Cod and helped me settle down in a shelter for the homeless, run by one of their friends. That day, I rented a bike for $40 and began my job hunt.

The shelter was a gathering of interesting personalities. Quite a number of its residents told me that they were proud to be homeless and unemployed. It was their choice. One of them, George, had features that were not too different from that of Michaelangelo's David. He was tall and strong, with shoulder-length hair and a canvas backpack. He told me that he was constantly on the road to discover himself and find *the* job. He further described to me how he had been disowned by his multi-millionaire father because of his heretic and anti-establishment ideology and his unruly behavior. At the end of the day, he would come back and announce to me, and our fellow shelter residents, that he had finally found the ideal job—cook's help in a family restaurant, or gas station attendant. The very next day, he would quit the newly-found ideal job, and continue his search.

Having been told by a supervisor that I was a student, working on my doctoral degree, several of the residents approached me to pick my brain about many esoteric subjects. To them, it was profound stuff.

One of them found a sheet of paper, scribbled something like $\psi \wp \Pi \Re \omega \Pi \varpi \Sigma \partial \notin \Omega \xi$ on the paper, claimed that he had discovered the script in a dream, and challenged me to decipher its meaning. I would work with them in good humor, but as hard as I tried, I couldn't make out for sure whether it was Chinese, Japanese, Arabic, Sanskrit, or a coded message sent by some friendly Martians, or a mixture of them all. Seeing that I was baffled, the discoverer and his friends would roar with hearty laughter. They were a fun crowd to hang out with.

The shelter was a rather neat place, too. The staff would hand you a set of clean sheets when you checked in every evening. Each room had about a dozen beds. There was a place to take a shower and all meals were free. You could have milk, donuts, and coffee for breakfast, and leftovers donated by restaurants for dinner. Then, in the middle of one night, one of the residents got up, stood over another resident who was

My Car Complex 23

soundly asleep, and peed right into his face. The victim of this nocturnal surprise attack woke up, jumped out of bed, and screamed bloody murder while going after his tormentor's throat, seeking nothing short of blood for revenge. It was only with the help of several rather muscular guys that the staff on duty that night succeeded in separating the two before anyone was seriously hurt.

By then, I had already found three jobs in Hyannis. I cooked potato chips full time on the 2nd shift: from 2:00 to 10:00pm. I did housekeeping at a Days Inn motel, making beds, changing sheets and vacuuming the littered carpets from 8:00 to 12:00 in the morning seven days a week. Finally, I flipped burgers and pushed orders at a Burger King restaurant on Saturday and Sunday afternoons and evenings.

With three incomes, I was able to rent a room and move out of the shelter.

Of these three jobs, the toughest was the one at the potato chips plant. When I first came to apply for the job, I peeked through a window glass and saw rows of darkish steaming work stations and macho men with towels tied around their foreheads working like slaves. "Are you sure you want this job?" the soft-spoken personnel manager looked at my bookish appearance and short stature and asked, in a concerned voice.

"Of course," I reassured her. I was eager to work and I wanted to start right away.

Every workday for the next two and half months, I would literally toil and sweat there like an indentured servant. I would stand by the side of a huge container that held more than 100 gallons of sizzling cooking oil. The oil percolated at nearly 400 degrees. My job was to churn sliced potatoes with a long, metal rake so that they would be cooked evenly and would not stick together. I sweated as if I were a soaking sponge that was being squeezed.

My coworkers—Americans, Irish college students, and new immigrants from India, Pakistan, and Thailand—much stronger than myself, would complain all the time about their sore muscles and back pains. They swore loudly that the work was not fit for humans. Often, the supervisor would ask me to stay after 10pm to clean up the greasy work stations with a high pressure water hose. By then, I was already dog tired.

Exhausted, I would dress in thick, clumsy protection gear,

and drag the heavy hose around, pumping steaming water into the work stations. The air would fill with thickly cloying moisture, making it extremely difficult, at times, for me to breathe. Sometimes, I would feel so weak that I was ready to drop. But the temptation of overtime at time-and-a-half the regular pay—$14.62 an hour, more than four times the minimum wage then—was not easy to resist. It made the four hour purgatory-like overtime well worth it. That summer, I lost 20 pounds even though I had no need to lose any weight.

Typically, when I was finally done, it would be around 2:00 in the morning. I would ride my bike home on the deserted country road. As I pedaled hard and raced up and down the road, I could hear the quiet murmuring, whistling and groaning in the midst of the tall New England trees that lined the road. Occasionally, a heart-piercing scream, or random swearing by drunkards and tramps, would emanate from some unknown spot. These sounds would echo eerily among the trees.

The worst was when it was drizzling or raining. The lenses in my glasses would collect water drops, blurring and eventually obscuring my vision. It was all I could do to hold the handlebars firmly, pedal hard and leave the rest to my intuition. Once I got home to the room I was renting, I would be totally exhausted and drenched. Despite it all, I would take a quick shower, go to bed, and try to catch a few hours of sleep before my shift at the Days Inn which would start at 8 o'clock. So it went, all summer long.

I think I may have passed the Kennedy's limousine one day on my way to work, and I did see tourists arrive in droves at this popular summer retreat. In fact, the Atlantic Ocean was just a short ride away from where I lived that summer. But I was so busy working that I never found time to take advantage of the beaches. Looking back at my situation, a car would have made a huge difference.

The night before I left, my landlady said to me, "Qi, you have been here two and half months and have not even been to the beach. Shame on you!" She insisted on driving me to the beach to have a look. When we—the landlady, a friend of hers, and me—got there, it was pitch dark and I couldn't see anything. I could hear the deep breathing and moaning of the ocean and feel its vast presence in the dark out there. Awed by the sublimity of it all, I declared, "Someday, I shall return with my wife and son and have a much better look at you!" That was the beginning and the end of my summer vacation.

III

SOON AFTER COMING BACK from my summer "vacation" in Cape Cod, I began to think about buying my first car. Buying a car is quite an exciting thing, but it can also be a headache. For me, the difficulty was not an emotional debate between new or old, imported or domestic cars. That decision was made rather simple for me by my bottom line. My bank statement dictated that I could afford only one kind of car: used, secondhand, or pre-owned, if you care to be more euphemistic.

Everyday, I read through the auto ads in the Classified section of the local newspaper. I would underline this ad, mark that and ask the owners questions concerning their cars: what make, model, year, mileage, price, automatic, manual, etc. Whenever I called, I would find my English too limited to engage in truly meaningful car talk. One thing I knew for sure, though: the car I was going to buy could not cost me more than $1000.

The real difficulty lay in the fact that I didn't yet own a car. It was a sort of catch-22 situation. I would have to purchase my very first car in order to join the rank and file of the car-owning class, yet without being a member of the car-owning class first I would not be able to go from Point A (where I was) to Point B (where the seller and his/her car were) to see and eventually to purchase my very first car. This predicament made my car purchasing experience rather frustrating at times.

Lao Liu from Xian took me to see a few cars, but I couldn't agree to any deals because they either 1) went beyond my price range, or 2) were in worse shape than Lao Wang's Toyota. The car I was looking for would be the first one in my entire life, and I didn't want to stoop as low as Wang had.

One day, I saw an ad in the paper for a 1979 Ford Fairmont: "4 door, 100,000 plus miles, great car for students, asking $980," claimed the ad. I called from a pay phone in the student cafeteria. After a few questions, I was satisfied and negotiated the price down to $650. Then, I asked Steve, who was doing the selling, to deliver the car to my place. "If everything is like what you said," I told him over the phone, "I'll write you a check."

When he pulled into a parking space in Cardinal Court—the graduate student compound where I had just gotten a one-bedroom apartment—that evening, my heart was beating as fast as if I was going on a blind date. The Fairmont had a grayish silver body, no obvious rust and four doors. It was fairly clean and responded crisply when you turned the ignition key. Steve opened up the hood and I looked and listened attentively, placing my head and ears as close to the engine as I dared—as if I could really tell.

Everything seemed to be in mint condition, so I wrote him a check and the car was mine.

When Steve had left, I sat alone in my car. I was a young man, spending the first night with his bride in the privacy of their bridal chambers. I touched her tenderly here and there. Then, I turned the ignition key on and off a few times, and every time the car would come alive with joy, its greenish lights glowing coquettishly in the dark. I was eager, my thirst was unquenchable and my heart was filled with wild expectation.

I got a copy of the Illinois State Drivers' Manual, studied the rules, took the written test, was granted a learner's permit, bought mandatory liability insurance and began to learn to drive in the university's parking lot. A few old timers—Chinese students who had a few years of driving experience under their belts—offered me some tips, and showed me a few moves. Then, Jim, an American college student, agreed to teach me more.

After a few rounds on the parking lot, Jim encouraged me to "hit the road." At first, I was a nervous wreck whenever I saw a car coming in the opposite direction, or when I saw that I was being tailgated. But I became bolder—gradually.

Every morning, when it was still dark, I would get up, sneak into the car and drive it out of Cardinal Court to the streets of a middle-class community not very far away. I remember the two early Saturday and Sunday mornings after I bought the car. The world was so quiet. Not a soul to be seen. The lush and well-manicured lawns were green and glistening with dew. Into this world of tranquillity came the intruder: me and my Fairmont.

I would go over the same routine again and again, back and forth: starting, turning, backing up and parking. Once I felt I had made enough noise on one street, I would move on to

My Car Complex

another, until it was broad daylight. How many good and innocent folks had been roused from their dreams on those two mornings! I was eager to the point of being thoughtless. About ten days later, I went for my road test. The officer from the Department of Motor Vehicles who administered my road test that day was a tall fellow with an expertly waxed, curly mustache. He turned out to be very laconic with no patience for any kind of conversation. Everything went smoothly until I made a wrong turn near the end of the test. The cause of the error could have been the fact that he was muttering out instructions through his nose and teeth so I didn't hear him clearly, or it could have been that I was too excited. The officer failed me and didn't want to listen to any explanations.

I came back the next day, and was fortunate enough to get a kinder-looking officer to administer the test. This time, I passed.

A week after I got my license, I was driving 70 miles an hour on Interstate 55 to Chicago, the ultimate rite of passage among the little community of Chinese graduate students at our Midwest university. I had to prove that I was finally a real driver by demonstrating my ability to handle the speed and traffic of the Interstate. When I first got on the highway, I was slow, going only 40 to 50 miles an hour. "Faster! Faster!" my friends in the passenger and back seats, who were witnessing my virgin solo trip to Chicago, urged as cars passed me impatiently.

I stepped on the gas pedal and the speed rose sluggishly to 70 miles an hour. I was almost breathless, my heart was ready to jump out of my mouth, and my hands gripped the steering wheel rigidly. It was not until quite a few minutes later that I got used to the speed and began to relax.

The most nerve-racking part of that trip was on Lake Shore Drive: six lanes going in the same direction, an ocean of automobiles of all kinds, shapes, colors, sizes and conditions. Some cars were much worse than mine; they were rusty, their muffler pipes trailing noisily on the road and coughing out puffs of thick, blue-gray smoke. The whole of Lake Shore Drive was like an endlessly enormous monster, twisting and moving its huge body uneasily and at a breathtaking speed.

My car was but an insignificant little scale, twisting and moving along passively. Some braver drivers, particularly the yellow cabbies, would weave in and out of lanes and cut right in front me without so much as using their turn signals. Occasionally, when I didn't move fast enough in changing lanes or closing up gaps, I would be honked at unceremoniously. I was nervous, but I stayed focused. I didn't dare to turn my head the slightest to cast even a glance at the shimmering waters of Lake Michigan under the bright, autumnal sun.

That day, I had passed the real driver's test and had become a real driver.

IV

WHILE ALL OF THIS car purchasing and driver's training was going on, I also got all the paperwork done to sponsor my wife and son to come and join me. I also applied for and got a one-bedroom apartment from the Office of Residential Life at the University. My wife and son experienced unforeseen difficulties in getting their part of the paperwork done, but eventually they succeeded in obtaining all the necessary official seals from various authorities. One day, in early December, my wife called and happily informed me that they were on their way.

Though by now I had almost two months of driving experience under my belt, I didn't completely trust myself or my old Fairmont yet. So I asked Lao Liu, a much more experienced driver, to drive me to O'Hare Airport with his not-too-old and much more dependable Toyota station wagon. When my family had safely landed, and we were dragging the luggage to Liu's car in the parking lot, my six-year-old son, who had been a loyal passenger on my bike back in China, asked sheepishly, "Dad, is this your car?" Oh, how I wished I had driven my own car to the airport that day, no matter how old or undependable it was!

Among the wives of Chinese graduate students in Cardinal Court, there was a saying that their men treated their cars as attentively and tenderly as if they were their concubines or mistresses. Their men worked ceaselessly on their car, cleaning, waxing, painting or changing oil and coolant water. Typically, it was their first car, bought with money saved a penny at a time. The car was usually at least ten years old, had more than 100,000 miles on it already and the body had varying degrees of rust. If we didn't take good care of them, we all justified, the cars would encounter trouble and cost much

My Car Complex   29

more to repair. Besides, boys being boys, our cars were just expensive toys for us to play with. Is that so wrong?

In Cardinal Court, there were 40-plus Chinese families, turning the graduate student compound into a mini-Chinatown of sorts. Every evening, you could see a group of them gathered around somebody's car. The subject of their conversation—more often than not—would be cars: who had just bought what kind of car at what cost, how to change this or fix that and so on. We could stand there and talk for hours. No wonder the wives were jealous.

Most of the wives came as *peidu*—a rather odd official Chinese category for spouses who came to keep their husbands company while they were pursuing their studies. The routine of a typical Chinese wife would go like this: in the morning, she would go to the local library to attend ESL lessons, usually survival English taught by volunteers; in the afternoon, she would go to a Chinese restaurant in town to work as kitchen help, dish washer, bus girl, cashier and even waitress if her English became fluent enough for her to handle taking orders and small talk with customers. She would not be done until sometime around 11:00 at night. At first, her husband would be her chauffeur, but gradually, she would struggle through the written test, learn to drive and pass the road test. Then she was cut loose to her own devices.

It is a truth universally acknowledged that husbands make lousy teachers for their wives. This is particularly true when it comes to teaching one's wife to operate a car. One of my friends became so impatient teaching his wife that she couldn't take it any more. So, I took over a big part of the teaching responsibility because I was a much more patient teacher when the student happened to be my friend's wife.

My wife, however, would complain about how she was traumatized by my impatience—even today whenever the subject comes up. She will also tell you, proudly, that she passed the road test on her first attempt. I know for whose ears that piece of information is really meant.

The old Fairmont made our life in the States much more manageable. In addition to getting my wife to work, son to school and the whole family to grocery stores for weekly shopping trips, I also drove it to Chicago to pick up newly-arrived Chinese students, or their wives and kids. I drove newcomers around to look for inexpensive apartments, to open their first checking or savings accounts, to buy groceries and other necessities. I even made money with the car by delivering pizzas at night.

That was the summer of 1992. In addition to taking two classes and teaching one section of freshman composition, I delivered pizza for the Pizza Hut located at the edge of town. Its service area included some downtown sections, and small villages and residences on the outskirts of town.

One time, I followed some delivery directions, only to arrive at a very old building outside of which the weeds had grown so tall that they reached up well beyond my knees. Not a single light was on.

The address indicated that the person who had placed the order was on the second floor. I turned on my flashlight, found a narrow and perilously steep stairway leading up to God knows where. The sound of my feet on the creaky wooden stairs echoed and amplified grotesquely in the darkness of the building. For a second, I had a clear consciousness of myself being a character in some second-rate Victorian detective or mystery novel.

Finally, I was at the top of the stairway. I found the right address on the second floor, and knocked on the door. Someone opened it and, against the flood of light pouring from inside, appeared a tall guy with a beer belly and tattoos on his chest and arms. "C'mon in," he invited, pleasantly.

"Thanks, I'm all right out here." As I answered, I caught glances of more than half a dozen bulging black trash bags lying all over the place inside his room. After he paid, I turned and walked with a measured pace down the stairs, but in my heart, I was running as fast as my legs could carry me. I was experiencing a fear much more real and acute than that of being a character in some morbid horror story. As soon as I got outside the building, I hurried to the safety of my car, started the engine and drove away. I had already heard quite a few horror stories of pizza delivery personnel being hurt, one of them involving a girl who had worked in the same restaurant.

The closest call, however, came one night when I was closing. I delivered my last order around midnight. It was a very dark night, and I was exhausted. Once I got on the highway, I raced back to the restaurant, breaking the speed limit law the whole way. Suddenly, I saw a stream of blinding lights coming fast in my direction, as if asteroids were raining down from the

My Car Complex 31

sky. I broke into a cold sweat: I was driving in the wrong direction! In a split of second, just when the first car was about to collide with mine head on, it swerved to the next lane, and the cars following it did the same, one after another. I was lucky. None of the drivers was dozing off or drunk that particular night on that particular stretch of the highway.

I slowed down and stopped on the shoulder. When the road was enveloped in darkness again, except for the two columns of light from my car, I turned around and started to go in the right direction. I sweated even more as the narrowly avoided consequences of my mistake began to sink in. I needed to be more careful.

The Fairmont's advanced age also caused me a lot of trouble. I don't know how many times it refused to start, particularly in winter, no matter how hard or patiently I tried. Its pickup was perennially sluggish. It took more than 30 seconds to achieve 60 miles per hour. Whenever I coaxed the car onto the highway and negotiated into the traffic, the cars behind me would have to brake. I almost got used to seeing drivers in my rearview mirror throw up their arms in anger, frustration and despair. Obligingly, I would step on the pedal harder, and the engine's roar became louder and more impressive, but the speed would only increase one mile at a time.

It broke down many times, too, rain or shine, winter or summer. How many good Samaritans stopped when they saw us stranded by the roadside, offering us a ride home or to the next gas station? I cannot count them all.

When I graduated in the Summer of 1993, and found a job at a college in Pennsylvania, we decided to sell the old car. It was a practical matter, really. I was concerned that the old Fairmont might not survive the long drive from Illinois to Pennsylvania.

When the eventual buyer came and got into the car, started the engine and began to drive it out of Cardinal Court, my son and I stood on the balcony of the second floor where our apartment was, bidding it farewell with our eyes. I became very sentimental, feeling like an ungrateful, treacherous, and unfaithful friend.

V

THE FAIRMONT was my first car, but certainly not the last. When my wife got her driver's license in the Summer of 1990, we bought another car, a 1984 Honda Accord. It cost us $3000. When I took the key from the dealer, the car looked almost new. It had just been washed, waxed, cleaned inside out, and was shining and sparkling. This car took us on many long excursions to Chicago, St. Louis, and all the way to Florida.

It caused us many problems, too: tire blowouts, timing belt failures, the list goes on. The worst was the day when I helped my wife move from Harrisburg, PA to the Bronx, NY for her first real job in the States. She had had enough of bussing tables and cleaning corporate offices, and finally got an offer from a molecular lab of a medical school where she could do what she had been trained to do and had been doing for years before coming to join me in this country.

It was an evening in January of 1994. That winter was one of the coldest, with frequent snow blizzards and sub-zero temperatures everyday. The highways were icy and slippery. On my way back home, when I was about to exit Interstate 80 to connect to Interstate 287, I felt the car slow down. No matter how hard I stepped on the gas pedal it refused to respond. Then, it stopped dead on the ramp. I got out of the car and looked back: cars—streams, no, galaxies of them, their headlights glaring—were stretching for miles and miles all the way to the sky; they had to slow down to a crawl, thanks to my car. Each one took the time to glance at me as they passed.

I hurried through snow and ice, climbed over a long and glaciated embankment, and found a gas station half a mile away. It had only one tow truck which was already busy towing cars like mine. I was told that they would not be able to get to my car for about two hours.

I sat in the gas station waiting, cowardly; I didn't have the guts to bring up in my mind again the picture of galaxies of cars being virtually stranded because of me. Good and innocent people were in a hurry to get home and bask in the warmth of their fireplaces, to settle some important business deals, or to rendezvous with their lovers or mistresses. They all became my victims.

My Car Complex 33

By the middle of the night, the towing truck had pulled my Honda off the ramp, and dropped it off at the gas station. I rented a car and drove another 120 miles through snow and ice back home where my 11-year-old son was waiting for me. The next day a mechanic called and said the clutch was totally gone and had to be replaced. It turned out to be a very expensive problem.

In the summer of 1994, we bought our third car, a new Honda Accord station wagon because my wife had found a job not far from home, and my parents were coming to visit us. It was with this car that we took my parents to visit many places: Washington D.C., New York, Philadelphia, Atlantic City and Gettysburg to name a few.

Close to the end of their visit, my father sat down to calculate how many times and how many miles he had ridden in the *xiaoqiche* during the six-month period. Numerous times and thousands of miles. How many times had he ridden in a *xiaoqiche* during his life back in China? He could count them on the fingers of only one hand. His lifetime means of transportation had been his bike. I felt a wave of warmth in my heart when I saw him sitting there, working on the numbers.

Today, a car is no less than a daily necessity in my eyes: a means for survival in this country. Its utility has far outstripped all of its mystique as once perceived by an elementary school boy 30 years before. At least I believe so.

Nonetheless, when I traded in the old 1984 Accord for a new Mazda not too long ago, I once again had the guilt-ridden sensation of betraying an old and loyal friend. Giving one last look at the abandoned, old Honda parked in front of the dealer's office, I turned the ignition key of the new Mazda and ran away.

Great Expectations

wang zi cheng long. This idiom encapsulates the hopes and dreams of almost all Chinese parents for untold generations. The first word in this idiom, *wang*, is a verb, which means more than its usual English translation, hope or expect, because it in its primary meaning involves the use of eyes, looking, watching, and gazing with eager expectancy. The second word, *zi*, means son, and the idiom in its traditional denotation refers to the male child exclusively, but because of recent social changes resulting from family planning policies, its reference has been broadened to include daughters. The English equivalent for the third word, *cheng*, is simply to become, or grow up to be. The third, *long*, means dragon; a totem for China (and Chinese civilization) and traditionally a symbol associated with Chinese emperors, *long* in this idiom stands for something extraordinary, e.g., exceptional talent, admirable prowess, enormous success, and glorious fame.

Did my parents, particularly my father, place such a high hope on me? I don't know. Born in the 1950s, I have an elder brother and a younger sister. If my father had cherished any hope close to *wang zi cheng long* for his sons, at least I could split the responsibility for living up to any expectations fifty-fifty with my brother.

I do remember, though, that when I was small—small enough to feel comfortable sitting in my father's lap—he wrote many Chinese characters on index cards for me to learn. Those cards served as a kind of primer for my early, childhood education. That was in the late 50s.

But Father was a busy man: busy running the schools that educated the poor, disadvantaged peasants' kids. He was normally so busy that he didn't have time to read to his children.

I knew Father was an important person in the community. Everyone addressed him respectfully as "Principal" or "Principal Qi." Everyday, he would prepare lessons, and work on important documents deep into the night. Half-asleep in bed, I would often listen to his nagging cough and the turn of pages.

By the time I was a second grader, I began to think about big things in my dimly-lit mind. I had seen the picture of Mao hanging in the center of the wall in our *tangwu*, a kind of family room, for more than half a dozen springs and falls. One day, I noticed that the forehead of Mao, the great leader who by then had acquired a halo much more glorious than that of any emperor in China's history, was of an extraordinary size: much bigger than that of an average man.

Drawing my own half-witted, second grade conclusions, I firmly believed that Mao's prominent forehead must be the fountain of his profound wisdom and celestial glory. So to make my young forehead appear bigger and more closely resemble Mao's, I found a pair of old scissors—which, by the way were not very sharp—and a mirror, and set to work.

Bending my head to gain a good view of my forehead in the mirror, I generously applied the scissors to my foremost, protruding locks. Because the scissors were so dull, I ended up pulling out most of it rather than cutting it. When I was finally done, I compared my hair with that of the great leader. I wasn't sure whether there was any resemblance. When my parents came home in the evening and noticed the work I had done and heard why I had done it, they didn't know whether to laugh or cry.

My aspirations to achieve greatness via the "shortcut" caused me more than some discomfort, though. A few days after my self-inflicted hair style, I was recommended by my elementary school to sit for an exam. The exam was for entrance to the Nanjing Foreign Languages school: a prestigious school whose mission was to prepare the best and the brightest of elementary school pupils for foreign service. At least this was its reputation then.

To sit for the exam, I had to have a photo for the application. My overexposed forehead would certainly make me less photogenic. So Father took me to a barber's in town, who picked up some hair from the floor and somehow stuck it on my forehead to cover up the area where I had applied the scissors. Then, we went directly to a photographer's just a few doors away from the barber's and had a picture taken. I have since lost the photo but to the best of my memory, the barber didn't do too bad a job, considering what he had to work with.

Nevertheless, I wasn't accepted to the school. To this day, I don't know why. Perhaps I did not exhibit any signs of linguis-

Great Expectations 37

tic talent. Or perhaps the school somehow got wind that my father, the principal of a middle school, was soon to be labeled a "capitalist-roader:" a moniker for which he would be locked up in a small, dark room in the back of the school yard, not to be "liberated" until several years later. I suspect, though, that it also had something to do with my forehead. With false hair on my forehead, and skinny as I was, I must have looked more like an impoverished impostor than a kid who had the promise of one day blossoming into a handsome diplomat, gloriously representing the People's Republic in the midst of foreign dignitaries.

In 1977, I went to college. My father was very excited. I was the first generation of college students in the whole Qi clan. My grandfather was a Confucian scholar of some note, a fine closet poet, and a *si shu xiang sheng*, an old-style private schoolmaster, and my father was a middle school principal. Still, neither had attended college. Father lost his chance to go to college when he was diagnosed with tuberculosis in high school. The newly-established Republic had to invest its limited educational resources on those few who would promise the greatest return.

Later, I was told that the evening after seeing me off to college at the train station, Father came back home and sat at the dinner table for a long time reminiscing about me, about what I did to help him during the Cultural Revolution.

For months in 1967, Father was locked up to help him repent and confess his "crimes." I was ten years old then, and would often go to visit him—almost daily. My mother wouldn't let my brother, three years older than I, go for fear that he might get into fights with the Red Guards who were no more than middle school kids. Mother herself couldn't go either because she had to devote herself to revolutionary production work, leaving home when it was still dark and coming back well after sunset.

I often brought along my little sister, who was only two or three years old then. As we trudged along the dirt road, we were often chased by barking dogs. At the school gate, the Red Guards who controlled the entrance would open whatever bowl or jar I was carrying to check for suspicious slips of paper with messages written in codes hidden deep in the rice and the simple vegetable dishes I had prepared. Sometimes the guards would show their uncompromising revolutionary spirit by spitting contemptuously into the bowl or jar before letting me and my sister in.

During those days, being Father's son meant more suffering than joy. One afternoon, the loudspeaker announced that my elementary school and Father's middle school, which were adjacent to each other, were going to have a joint struggle meeting against him. He had already been labeled a "three-anti bad element," which meant he was anti-the-Party, anti-the-people, and anti-socialism. I was scared. Should I stay and see my beloved Father being struggled with? No. I made up my mind.

While the middle-aged male homeroom teacher was still talking and instructing the pupils on what to do during the meeting, I made a dash for the door, ran out, and ran towards the school gate. I don't know whether the teacher gave the word or not, but several big bullies in the class gave chase, catching me before I had reached the other side of the gate. They grabbed my arms, pulled them far back, and forced my body into a posture called *zuo fei ji,* flying the airplane, a kind of cruel punishment popularly used during those days. Then, they dragged me to the office of one of the rebel corps commanders. He was a teacher who had been exceptionally kind to me before the Cultural Revolution started. He began to lecture me on the politically correct course that a son like me should take.

"Now, why did you try to run away?" he asked, his eyes looking at me up and down several times.

"My father is a good man," I answered, teary-eyed.

"How do *you* know?" the teacher questioned, sarcastically.

"Well, he has often told me to study hard Chairman Mao's works."

"Well," he paused a second, "even bad people sometimes pretend. . . "

So there was no escaping the struggle meeting.

In the center of the school's playground was a dirt platform, upon which were placed several tables. These tables were flanked by teachers and students wearing bright red bands on their left arms. Stretching across the two poles planted on either side of the platform, for all to see, was a big banner denouncing my Father in large characters.

Sitting among my classmates and hundreds of other teachers and pupils, I saw my Father being dragged onto the platform, his head forced down in submission. Speakers would march onto the platform one after another, going over the list of crimes Father allegedly had committed.

One of the worst of his crimes was a comment he made when Jiang Qing—Mao's wife—appeared for the first time in a photo in the *People's Daily*. Father, who had never heard of Jiang Qing before, had mentioned something about the possibility of her basking in the glory of Mao, an innocent yet unfortunate remark which became an entry in a secret notebook kept by a teacher who harbored a grudge against Father.

From that day on, I was to witness many more such struggle meetings. Sometimes, Father was forced to kneel on broken glass, sometimes they hung a heavy blackboard on his neck with thin wire that obviously cut into his neck. One night, Father later told me, they got into his room and beat him with a truncheon to force him to confess to more crimes, and ask for forgiveness.

Besides going to visit him while he was incarcerated, I did another thing to defend his honor.

One late afternoon, the western part of the sky was blood red. The heads of the sunflowers that grew along the edges of the country road, hung low with their fleshy seeds. When I heard the much-dreaded drums and gongs in the distance, I knew that they were coming. So I ran home and shut the door.

The procession drew near and stopped outside our home. Through a hole in the door, I could see Father. He was wearing a tall cone-shaped hat. His body was wrapped in big-character posters. While the struggle session was going on, Father had to beat the gong and shout slogans denouncing himself. Then, they marched him in this humiliating parade to other parts of the community.

After a while, when I couldn't hear any noise outside, I opened the door. What greeted my eyes on the wall of our house were big-character slogans written in black ink on large sheets of white paper: "Down with. . .!" "Deep Fry. . .!" "Club to Death. . .!" Father's name in these slogans was checked with a big red cross, meaning he had been sentenced to death for his high crimes.

I didn't like those sinister-looking posters on the wall. Particularly, I didn't like to see my beloved Father's name being juxtaposed with those violent words. I decided to act. I found a basin, and began to run back and forth between a little pond and the wall, pouring one basinful of water after another on the posters. In between basinfuls of water, I did my best to deface the posters, tearing at corners and poking at them with a dried twig, fallen from the tall toon. The result? When I was finished, the posters were coming off the wall in tattered pieces, inky water was dripping everywhere, and nobody, I mean nobody, could see Father's name in them anymore.

When Mother came back that evening, and saw what I had done, she was worried. "What will happen if they come back and see this?"

"I'll just tell them that we had a terrible thunderstorm," I answered, still elated with my bold accomplishment.

I've always known there was a special bond between Father and me, and he had great expectations for me. I promised myself that I would live up to those expectations.

When I started college as an English major, I was behind many of my classmates. While some of them had already done a tour of duty in *English 900*, a popular, multi-volume English textbook among students in China at the time, I was still struggling with the alphabet. But I knew I had to *zheng qi*, or try my best to bring honor to my family, particularly to Father.

Like the proverbial turtle, I was humble, stubborn and persistent, and I was rewarded for being such: I graduated from college with top honors and was assigned a teaching position in the same college. That was in the early 1980s. At that time, some institutions of higher learning began to enroll graduate students again, tentatively, after graduate programs had been discontinued for many years. Since the graduate programs of these few institutions were very modest and capable of accommodating only a handful of students, only the best among college graduates could apply, and the best had to compete against the best in order to get in. Being accepted by a graduate program would unmistakably represent the epitome of one's social and academic success.

Father never said, "Xiao Hua, you should try for graduate school," but I knew that he'd be very happy if I tried, and he'd be much happier if I succeeded. I knew I would be much happier, too.

So I prepared. Everyday for about half a year, I would read deep into the night, never bothering to waste my time on things like movies, or social activities.

Then, I applied and sat through a three-hour exam. I was grilled on Shakespeare, Johnson, Coleridge, Saussure,

Great Expectations　　　　　　　　　　　　　　　　41

Chomsky, Freud and William the Conqueror. I scribbled on for the whole three hours. When it was over, I remember that my right wrist was stiff with exertion.

Out of over 100 ambitious young scholars nationwide who were applying to the same graduate program, I was one of the lucky five who were eventually accepted. I lived a puritan life for the next three years—the required length of study for graduate programs in China then—and graduated with a master's degree in 1985.

When I was done, I vowed I'd never go back to school as a student. I had had more than my share of student life. I began to devote myself to college teaching. I also began to publish in my own field. I thought I was doing okay, as a budding young scholar.

At that time, Ph.D. programs were virtually unheard of, and master's degree holders among college and university faculties were still valued as national treasures. By the late 1980s, however, things began to change.

More and more college graduates were streaming out of China to study abroad. At first, I thought I could follow my chosen path instead of jumping on the bandwagon with everybody else. I could still be successful by being a good teacher and by writing and publishing as a scholar.

Gradually, however, I too became restless. I wanted to know what it was like to study in an English-speaking country, specifically in the United States. I wanted to study under the guidance of well-known American professors. The attraction of such a prospect was three-fold: a potential doctoral degree in my field; an opportunity to experience life and culture firsthand in the United States; and a chance to make some money so that when I came back I wouldn't have to bend my proud back to anyone for the sake of a livelihood.

Again, Father never so much as said that I should try. But whenever the topic came up in our family get-togethers, Father would be full of praises for those daring young folks whose adventures in foreign countries were reported in the newspapers in glowing terms. I knew that it would make him very happy if I could be one of them.

So I climbed to the top floor of the municipal library, searched in the *Peterson's Guide for Graduate Studies in the U.S.*, copied down pages of names and addresses, and sent out more than a dozen application letters. While waiting for responses, I took the required TOEFL and GRE tests, having registered for them with American dollars borrowed from relatives. Again, I was lucky: I was accepted and offered a full graduate teaching assistantship.

Father's letters followed me to the States, and everywhere I moved. In every letter, he would write earnestly how proud he was of me, how other teachers at his school and how his neighbors were full of praises. He encouraged me to continue to work hard and never become conceited or complacent. He also urged me to pay attention to my health because without good health everything else would become meaningless. I still have all of the letters he wrote me since I arrived in the States. There are hundreds, all neatly arranged in a big binder. Whenever I open the binder and turn the pages, I can hear Father's voice talking to me again.

He even wrote some poems—although he wasn't much of a poet in the technical sense—to express his happiness, pride and expectations. He missed me, too. But in his eyes, pursuing a doctoral degree in the United States meant that I was doing something truly important.

Later, when my first book, a co-translation of a Thomas Hardy novel, was published in China, Father went to the publisher, got more than two dozen copies of the book, and gave a copy to each of our relatives and to each of my elementary and middle school teachers. It didn't matter to him at all whether the recipient of the book had heard of Hardy, or whether they had any interest at all in foreign literature. My name was on the cover of a published book. That was all that mattered.

When my mother told me about this, I shook my head, knowing full well that Father was erroneous in assuming that everybody else would share the same excitement or pride as he felt for my little accomplishment. But in my heart, I felt a comforting warmth. I had proved myself a worthy son and had not disappointed him. When he came to visit us in 1994, after six years of not having seen each other, the first thing he took out of his suitcase was a copy of that book.

Besides the usual dream of *wang zi cheng long*, Father, in some ways, realized his own dreams which had been dashed by tuberculosis and by the class his family was designated into right after 1949. Before that year, my grandfather had owned a small grocery store that supported his big family. Because of this, the family was classified as "upper middle peasant," two tiers above that of the starkly poor "poor peasant."

Great Expectations 43

For this reason, Father—much more talented than I am—was never really trusted by his superiors or by the Party. He had been used as a work horse, but had always been conveniently passed over for promotion. I know that I have not achieved anything anywhere close to "enormous success" or "glorious fame," but Father's gentle prodding has been fueling me all along. In that sense, I have always been a success in his eyes, and this thought constantly comforts me since he passed away in 1995.

As a father myself, I have had my share of the *wang zi cheng long* dream, too. In light of the "one family, one child" policy, I told my wife that I didn't mind much whether our child—the only child we would be allowed to have—was a boy or a girl. My parents and everybody else in the family said much the same. We were educated. We were enlightened. We were above the old, backward way of thinking that treasured boys and trashed girls.

But, deep down in my heart, and deep down in the heart of the big family headed by Father, we were hoping for a boy. My brother had a daughter, born to his small family three years before. My niece, though still very young, showed signs of being gifted. She would be a worthy granddaughter to my father. Nevertheless, we were hoping for a male offspring to carry on the Qi family name in my father's line. At least it would be a nice balance.

When my wife gave birth to our son—I was told later because, at that time, I was far away in another city—Father was filled with so much joy that for days he walked with a joyful spring in his step.

I assumed the honor and responsibility of naming my son. I took this business seriously because in his name would be invested my dream and the dreams of the big Qi family. I looked through dictionaries and encyclopedias and finally, after much deliberation, settled down on the word *hao,* a Chinese character with rather complex strokes.

My criteria for the name were three-fold. First, it had to be sonorous, and *hao* fit the bill because its utterance involves opening your mouth wide, and releasing air, held deep in your lungs, with some force. Second, it had to have some significant meaning. The denotation of *hao* is great, vast and boundless, which certainly expressed my—my family's—hope that this child would grow up to be a person of enormous intelligence, knowledge and talent. Third, it could not be common. The *hao*

I chose was rare, and had a much more complex stroke pattern than another *hao* of the same sound and meaning that is more commonly adopted.

I must say, I have been a much less gentle and patient father to Hao, than my father was to me. I have played my role much more aggressively and clumsily. Of the many blunders I have made as a father, the worst was forcing music on him.

When Hao was about three years old, my wife and I went to the music store in the center of town, fought our way up to a very crowded counter, took out a bundle of money from the inside pocket of my winter coat—it had taken me about ten years to save up that money—paid the clerk, and carried an electronic keyboard home. We would have bought a piano if we could have afforded it. The teacher we found for him was a professor who taught in the music department of the university where I also taught.

With the mandatory family planning policy, every family can have only one child and every family wants that child, boy or girl, to be a prodigy. So parents spend a lot of time and money on making that dream come true: taking them to drawing and music lessons, teaching them to recite poetry, teaching them advanced math, chess, what have you.

Newspapers and magazines are filled with stories of young babies, one or two years old, who have learned one or two thousand Chinese characters, can recite dozens of classic poems, can write beautiful calligraphy, and so on. Young parents look to their own child, and hope their child will turn out to be just as gifted and famous—if not more.

So, besides home lessons in language and math, Hao began his keyboard lessons. Everyday I would make sure that he practiced. If his attention strayed after ten or twenty minutes, I'd scold him. I'd expect him to remember a piece by heart after only a few attempts, and to be able to play it expressively.

Quick in learning and mastering new things would certainly be a sign of genius. Sometimes, I'd hold a ruler in my hand and when he repeated an error he had made before, I'd hit his fingers with the ruler; though the hit was rather light, it must have hurt him very much. Even when his paternal and maternal grandparents were visiting and waiting for the Chinese New Year's feast to begin, I would not be flexible. I'd keep him in the next room with the door shut, and would not let him out

Great Expectations 45

until he had finished the practice session satisfactorily. He made good progress, but how many drops of tears he had shed during those days?

Luckily for him, I left for the United States to pursue my own dream. Since my wife was very busy and no one was available to supervise his practice, his music lessons slackened gradually until they stopped altogether.

Hao came with his mother to join me close to the end of 1989. During the first few years he was in the States, we were extremely busy. I had to juggle being a student, a graduate teaching assistant, a waiter in both Chinese and American restaurants and various other responsibilities. Hao, on his part, was struggling with a totally new language and culture, though after less than one year, his verbal score in the Iowa Tests of Basic Skills was above the 50th percentile for his grade. His math was in the 99th percentile.

By the fall of 1992, however, my wife and I became concerned about his music education again, and about having been neglectful in this area. A well-educated person, in the classic Chinese sense, should be adept in many disciplines. He should be a master of *qin, qi, shu, hua,* music, chess, calligraphy and drawing or painting.

"Do you want to resume your music lessons with a piano teacher?" I asked Hao, tentatively. He hesitated.

After a long, thoughtful silence, he answered, "I will, if you don't beat my fingers with a ruler anymore." I acknowledged that I had fouled up before, and I promised him that this would never happen again if he agreed to resume the lessons.

"Deal," he said, uncertainly.

For 300 dollars, we bought a very old and heavy upright; it took six of my friends to move this cumbersome thing into our second-floor apartment. We found him a teacher through a music store in town, and I began to drive him to his weekly lessons in our very old, Ford Fairmont. He was 9 years old then.

Because of the long lapse, Hao had to start all over again. While I tried hard to keep my side of the bargain, he was getting back his feel and came to enjoy taking piano lessons more and more.

When we moved to Pennsylvania, we bought another piano and found another teacher for him right away. No time was lost. As he got better and better, he'd occasionally talk about majoring in music in college. A fancy we didn't share, and discouraged in as diplomatic and subtle a way as we could manage. We knew that it was too late for someone like him to seriously contemplate a career in music.

Now Hao is fifteen, much taller than I am, and more intelligent. As a 10th grader, he's doing great in all subjects, is actively involved in school's newspaper, various clubs and has real ambition. I don't know what is the driving force behind all this. I don't know whether making his parents proud is even a factor at all.

While we can talk about a lot of things together, he is more reluctant when it comes to sharing his work with me. Perhaps he still has memories of his early music lessons. Perhaps it is because he knows that whenever he shares his writings with me, I'll always follow a brief praise of some good points with the big transitional word, "but..." He came to hate this word. But I know he has grown up and is pretty much on his own now. I should let go.

In a PSAT he took a few months ago, he scored a perfect 800 in math. Which was really more than I had expected. I know that such tests are not accurate or reliable in measuring one's true learning and ability, and thus should not be used to predict future success. Nevertheless, it was an impressive score. I should be proud. His PSAT verbal score was 650. Good enough for a 10th grader, but when I looked at the errors he made, I knew where he needed work.

While debating whether to offer help, I received an email from a Chinese friend of mine. He talked about his daughter whose scores of standard tests were: SAT I Verbal: 740; Math 780; SAT II Writing: 740; Math II 790; Physics 750.

According to her father, a very devoted and loving father, however, the scores were "okay, but not very good." Why should Chinese parents have such unreasonably high expectations for their children, and how hard should Chinese children work to meet their parents' expectations?

Being caught between two cultures, two languages, their Chinese parents and mainstream American society, they have enough to deal with already. Not that these pairs mentioned are always at odds with each other, but the danger of a child being rejected by both is real. They could be rejected by their parents' culture about which their knowledge is inadequate, and they could be rejected by the mainstream culture simply because of their Chinese identity, the most apparent features of which would be the color of their hair and skin.

Great Expectations

People of my generation, when rejected by the mainstream culture, have traditionally fallen back upon our cultural roots. At least, we were born and grew up in our own culture, and had lived and worked in that culture for many years before coming to the United States.

So, I suppose I have decided to lighten up and not to heap any more stress on my son.

On the morning of Christmas Eve this year, 1998, it suddenly occurred to me that being preoccupied with taking care of my own things, I hadn't prepared a gift for Hao. Desperate, I jumped into the car and raced to a bookstore in the local mall. I looked and looked and finally settled on a book titled, *The 100: A Ranking of the Most Influential Persons In History.* Listed among the hundred are Muhammad, Christ, Buddha, Confucius, Plato, Columbus, Darwin, Newton and Einstein. These people were truly dragons, having had enormous intelligence, success, fame and influence.

Was the choice somewhat Freudian? Nooooo. But, it may not have been completely accidental, either.

So much for the expectations and dreams all parents in the world cherish for their children.

A Dark-haired, Yellow-Faced English Professor

AUGUST, 1995. SEATTLE INTERNATIONAL AIRPORT. I was waiting in one of those long customs lines. I had just returned from a whirlwind trip to China to visit my dear Father who was fighting lung cancer. I was not in the best mood. Finally, it was my turn, and I presented my documents to an officer from the Office of Immigration and Naturalization Services.

"What do you do for a living in the U.S.?" asked the officer. He was smartly dressed in a uniform with an eagle insignia. His voice was businesslike, but nevertheless carried unmistakable authority.

"Teaching," I answered, respectfully.
"What do you teach?"
"English."
"What level?"
"College."

He looked up from my documents and stared at me for a second as if to make sure my face matched the photo in the passport. A cloud of doubt and irritation floated across his face.

"Who says you're qualified to teach English in the U. S.?" he questioned.

"My doctoral degree in English says so," I snapped back proudly.

The officer didn't say anything more. He stamped my passport and let me in.

I have encountered scenes similar to the one sketched above many times before and many times since. The only difference is that the INS official was more honest and direct.

Every time someone—whether they are American or Chinese—asks me what I do for a living, and I give the above answer, I would notice something along the lines of "Wow! Isn't that something? But. . ." written all over their faces. I would feel apologetic as if I owe the interlocutor an explanation.

As a result of historical circumstances—the ending of the protracted Cultural Revolution, the opening of China after

−49−

decades of isolation, the many tragedies at Tiananmen Square—known to all, tens of thousands of Chinese students have come to the U.S., studied, graduated, found employment and settled down in this country. Not a small number of them have competed their way into Academia in a tight job market. In fact, if you open up the catalogue of almost any institution of higher learning, from the top-notch Ivy League research universities down to much smaller junior or community colleges, you'll find more than a few mainland Chinese names listed in the faculty pages. You can spot them right away because of the *Pinyin* system used in their names. The subjects they teach extend to almost every branch of the knowledge tree, though most of them are in the fields of science and technology. Occasionally, though, you'll find one or two anomalies: tenure track or already tenured Chinese English professors.

These are the few graduate students from China who have not "defected" from English to fields such as Applied Computer Science, Education, Library Science, etc. where employment prospects were felt to be more alluring. This at least was true at the university in the Midwest where I pursued my doctoral degree in English. Out of more than a dozen Chinese students in the English program, only 3 or 4 stayed and graduated. They were awarded for their fidelity, though: all of them eventually found tenure-track positions.

Are we qualified? Can we handle the rigors of teaching English to American college students? We, of all people, to whom English is only a second, or more accurately, foreign language? Plus the fact that some of us began to learn English rather late?

I began my English studies very late. According to most linguists, I was already past the critical stages for language development. All physiologically and psychologically normal children—these language pundits have announced—manage to become proficient speakers of their native language by the age of four or five, even without instruction. Yet this startling special, innate talent for language acquisition tends to drop off around the onset of puberty.

I didn't begin to learn English until 1977, when I was almost twenty. Of course, by then I had already hit puberty. If I hadn't by then, I think I would have been in deep, deep trouble.

Starting to learn another tongue when I had lost not only my pre-puberty innocence, but also much of that special talent for language acquisition, was certainly not very encouraging.

A Dark-haired, Yellow-Faced English Professor 51

Of course, I knew that there was such a thing called "English" before I celebrated my 20th birthday. I had even learned, during my middle school years, to mimic English. I could say slogans like, "Long Live Chairman Mao!" and "Power grows out of the gun barrel!"

I didn't have an inkling of clue as to what those two strings of unearthly sounds really meant.

The night before taking a spoken English test, as part of a battery of college entrance exams, I went back to my middle school English teacher, asking her to show me how to pronounce the alphabet more English-like. What else could I do to cram for this once-in-a-lifetime test which would determine my future? Thanks to this last-minute effort, I was able to recite the alphabet from beginning to end without stumbling once during the exam the next morning. Quite a tour de force, at least in my own estimation of the situation.

My redemption that day was a native desire to learn. This desire rescued me from total disgrace, and earned me a seat in a college classroom. To make sure that there was still an iota of hope for me, foreign language professors from Beijing, Nanjing, and other top universities joined forces and launched a frontal assault on me with their most lethal weapons: their lips, tongues, teeth, noses and vocal chords.

They fired away with pairs of sounds such as [t] [d], [k] [g], [s] [z], much in the manner of magicians or clowns—at least it seemed theatrical to me then. One of the professors would bite his lower lip with his upper teeth, hold his breath for a suspenseful half second, and then suddenly force the air to pass through the barricaded passage: [v]! I was not ready to be crushed by the blow of hot air. I was alert. My eyes were wide open, and I was all ears. I followed suit: bit my lower lip with my upper teeth, held my breath for a suspenseful half second, and then suddenly forced the air to pass through the barricaded passage by applying some air pressure with my young lungs: [v]!

Another professor would shoot out pairs of words such as "light/night," "life/knife," and "like/Nike," for me to imitate. I found out later that this was to see whether I was able to distinguish between [l] and [n]. The former is a sound produced by touching the upper palate with the tip of the tongue, and the latter is a nasal sound produced with a vibration of the nose. Folks in Nanjing, my hometown, are notorious for their inability to tell [l] from [n]. I passed that test, too.

So I went to college. There, I found out to my dismay that some of my classmates were already well beyond the alphabet. Quite a few of them had already completed a tour of duty of the *English 900* published by MacMillan. This textbook is built around 900 core English sentences, from the simplest "Good morning, sir," "Come in, please," "This is my umbrella," to rather complex sentences such as "You should take an umbrella with you because the sky is overcast with dark clouds and it never rains but pours here."

I remember one rather tall and handsome fellow, proudly singing "Row, Row, Row Your Boat!" and "Singing Our Socialist Motherland" in English before the entire class of 130 students. How many of my female classmates secretly fell in love with him, I don't know.

I suspect that most of these folks hadn't had to pack up and go to the countryside to receive "re-education" from the peasants. They most likely hadn't had to haul carts, or bend their backs low to toil and sweat in the muddy rice fields that were filled with leeches and stinking cow manure. These classmates obviously didn't know what it was like to have several greedy leeches bury their heads deep into legs and feet with the midsummer sun, scorching overhead.

What was I going to do? I developed a rather simple strategy. Every morning, I would get up very early, tiptoe out of the dorm, and sneak into the misty orchard right behind the college campus. There, caressed by the quiet peach and apple trees, I practiced aloud: [t] [d], [k] [g], [f] [v], [s] [z], "Good morning, sir," "Come in, please," "This is my umbrella," all the way to "You should take an umbrella with you because the sky is overcast with dark clouds and it never rains but pours here." Over an hour later, when I tiptoed back to the dorm, with frost, dew, or raindrops in my hair and eyebrows, some of my roommates would still be wandering in their personal dreamlands.

At night, when the lights in the dorm were turned off, I would cover myself completely in the cotton-padded quilt, and go over the list of new words and sentence patterns, with the aid of a flashlight. Breathing could get a bit difficult inside the airtight quilt. In fact, it was inside this airtight quilt that I often tutored a male classmate of mine who was experiencing more difficulties with the lessons. No homosocial or homoerotic notions whatsoever ever crossed my (or our) mind(s), though the situation may seem compromising upon review. The truth is, we did not even know that such words or such notions exited in English.

A Dark-haired, Yellow-Faced English Professor

By the end of the first semester, my name had quietly crept into the ranks of the class's top students. It would remain there for the next few years.

NEVERTHELESS, WHEN I CAME TO THE U.S. in January, 1989, to pursue a doctoral degree in English, I had never dreamed that one day I'd stay on to be a professor of English in a college classroom. Indeed, I wasn't even sure if I would be able to perform my duties as a graduate teaching assistant, but in order to obtain a visa from the American embassy in Shanghai, I needed the full teaching assistantship.

It was an extremely cold winter. Ice and thick snow covered everything for weeks that year. I watched my own breath crystallize in the air as I walked into Dr. Woodson's office on that winter day.

This was the first time I met him, though we had communicated via letters for quite a while before meeting in person. His office was spacious. Several huge bookcases filled with hardcover editions threatened to touch the ceiling.

He was sitting behind a large executive desk. His healthy face looked much healthier due to the heater that worked furiously to keep the cold out. His eyes were big, wide open and alert, radiating a mixture of warmth, curiosity, care and sarcasm. He reminded me of an experienced hunter who has figured out his prey's every move and is at the ready.

His hands, crossed over each other, rested comfortably on his bulging belly. His thumbs chased each other, clockwise and counterclockwise continuously, as if to help him cope with the boredom of it all.

After an exchange of pleasantries, I confessed to him all of my anxieties concerning my upcoming teaching responsibilities. As far as most English graduate programs are concerned, "teaching assistant" is quite a misnomer because you are not an assistant to anyone at all, fulfilling your hour requirement by simply observing classes or grading homework or papers. You are actually teaching. You design the syllabus and lecture and grade papers. It's the real thing.

"Do you think I can handle it?" I asked. My eyes burned. I was still jet-lagged.

"Well, I guess if those farmers knew that a non-native speaker was teaching their sons and daughters college English, they wouldn't be too thrilled," he rounded his lips, and mumbled through his teeth, " 'Is dis a joke or something? That's like throwing our money away!'" He winked at me. Right away his face looked serious again: "I have full confidence in you, Qi. Your records tell me that you can handle it."

"Oh, please don't bring up my records, or TOEFL and GRE scores," I thought to myself. I had taken them in the spring of 1988. The evening before the test, my wife had cooked a wonderful meal. Perhaps I had had more than my share. Anyway, I finished off the meal with a few cups of strong tea.

That night, it was "Sleepless in Nanjing."

While the whole city was buried deep in sleep, my mind was as translucent as the water in my childhood pond where I used to sit—at its edge—and count each hair on the heads of shrimp that lay half-hidden between the rocks.

When I got up in the morning, my mind was foggy. In the test center at Nanjing University, I could not get rid of the fog no matter how hard I shook my head. I put the test headphones on, and began the section on listening comprehension.

I was comprehending and filling the ovals on the answer sheet with confidence until I got to the last mini-talk where a professor was explaining the schedule of classes for the upcoming spring semester to a student. I was following the explanation all right when all of a sudden I was hit by a wave of drowsiness. My mind blacked out and my life suddenly stopped—for a few seconds.

When I came to again, the student, satisfied with the advice he got, was saying goodbye to the professor. As a result of my dozing off—though only a few seconds, I stared at two of the questions and could not recall any relevant information. Clueless, I darkened the first oval for both questions with the #2 pencil and moved on to other sections of the test. Of course, I failed to reach the goal I had set for myself.

Having learned a lesson, I had a very simple dinner and avoided tea altogether the evening before the GRE test. Regardless, It was dejavu and another Sleepless in Nanjing: the same translucent water throughout the night, and the same heavy fog in the morning. This time, though, I had no excuses.

Just as with the test, there was no backing out of this assistantship now. On the first day of my second semester, I walked into a classroom on the second floor of the Stevenson Hall where all the writing classes were taught. On that day, my college teaching career in the United States was launched.

My heart beat wildly. I had difficulty breathing. My vision was

A Dark-haired, Yellow-Faced English Professor 55

blurry. All I saw as I walked in was computers—20 or 30 of them; 286? 386? I can't recall now—arranged around the walls and in the middle of the room. And 20 or 30 pairs of eyes—blue? brown? dark?—turning around and looking in one direction: at me. What was in their eyes? I was too self-conscious to notice. Later, reading their journals I found out that they were as nervous on that day as I was, if not more. For most of them, it was their first class on their first day in college. Away from their parents, their boyfriends or girlfriends, their familiar environment. They had a lot to prove, too. The only difference is that at the moment I was caught in the spotlight, on center stage and expected to perform. They were the spectators.

It was my job as a kind of director, to turn these spectators into actors and actresses. Close to the end of the semester, some of them told me that they were surprised—some said they were actually disappointed—on that first day when they saw a young, dark-haired "Asian" walk in and introduce himself as their English professor. Most couldn't tell a Chinese from a Korean or a Japanese.

The profile of a college professor they had had in their mind—pieced together from Hollywood movies, maybe?—was a distinguished looking middle-aged scholar—more likely male than female—whose regalia would include a head of gray hair and a pair of expensive glasses. I did wear glasses, but I failed to fit the bill otherwise.

I can't exactly recall how I stumbled through that first class. I did introduce myself to the class, asked the students to introduce themselves and explained the syllabus. Then I told them how to turn on their computers, access the word processor and showed them some basic commands and keystrokes. I let them write and experiment with different fonts and sizes, copying, cutting, pasting, saving and printing. Suddenly, the room came alive.

I was actually handling it all right.

My syllabus was an adaptation of a few sample syllabi provided by the English department. As to computers, I had only heard of them. I had never actually seen one. During the previous semester, I obtained a book of instructions, and began to learn about them.

I could type at a fairly decent speed, having learned to type on an ancient-looking Underwood typewriter which was about a foot tall and 50 pounds. Its ribbon was worn out and so dry that you had to strike the keys really hard to leave a legible mark on paper. It was on this typewriter that I—between coaxing, hitting, shaking, and cussing—completed most of the papers before their due date during my master's program.

One day in the department's learning center, having figured out how to turn a computer on and off, and launch the word processor, I began to type away. I was excited and eager to show off my typing skills. My ten fingers danced gracefully and in rapid cadence on the keyboard. "Qi, are you playing the piano?" I turned around, and looked into Dr. Woodson's big eyes. He winked at me. His eyes betrayed his curiosity and no little sarcasm. I quickly realized that typing on the keyboard did not require anything close to that level of gracefulness.

It was 1989. Even in America, the PC was not as much a household necessity as it is today. Windows, multimedia and the Internet were unheard of outside Silicon Valley. Most of the students in my class were using computers for the first time. In fact, many didn't even type well. A few could only use their index fingers, typing with a slow staccato while moving their heads left and right to look for the right keys. This method is much in the fashion of *xiao ji chi mi*, little chickens picking up scattered rice on the ground, one bit at a time.

This, however bad it sounds, was a boost to my confidence. Another boost came from the few students who were a few steps ahead of everybody else with computers. They were always happy to pitch in, and became the classroom troubleshooters. With their help, I survived my first class.

Indeed, students were very understanding and cooperative that semester. I was learning to swim by swimming, and we were helping each other so that nobody drowned. In the meantime, I was observing classes taught by veteran graduate students, and taking courses on composition theories and pedagogy. The English department was running workshops and training sessions which I attended. What was unsettling to me—at least, at first—were the humiliatingly low grades veteran graduate assistants and the director of the writing program were giving to sample student essays which followed the so-called five-paragraph scheme:

Introduction:	Paragraph 1
Body:	Paragraph 2
	Paragraph 3
	Paragraph 4
Conclusion:	Paragraph 5

A Dark-haired, Yellow-Faced English Professor

First off, even though I had a master's degree in English, I had never had any exposure to writing theory. Secondly, any decently educated Chinese would know a basic 4-part formula known as *qi chen zhuan he* in Chinese: *qi* prepares the reader for the topic; *chen* introduces and expands the topic; *zhuan* turns to a direction that seems unrelated to the topic, but is somehow relevant; and *he* sums up the essay. In its original classic expectations, this 4-part formula is quite dissimilar to the English 5-paragraph scheme. On a superficial level, they seemed to resemble each other, so I was at a loss. What was wrong with essays having such clear organization?

As I became a more critical reader and more experienced teacher, I realized that while there was nothing intrinsically wrong with such a structure, many students tended to regard writing as no more than going through the motions in the 5-paragraph scheme. I began to understand that writing is a complex and intellectually demanding problem-solving process. Good writing involves critical reading, critical thinking, gathering, analyzing and synthesizing data, reaching your own conclusion and communicating to the intended readers effectively. It requires a mature understanding of the dynamics between the subject, the audience and the purpose of any given rhetorical situation, and effective use of a variety of strategies in the whole process of writing: inventing, planning and drafting, revising, and editing and proofreading. This new understanding was quite exciting to someone coming from a society that was quite structured and did not encourage explorations beyond the defined limits.

This understanding of writing would be the basic framework of almost all of my writing instructions in the subsequent years. One of the writing assignments I developed when I began to teach as a tenure-track professor was about affirmative action.

The assignment involves the use of a videotape about discrimination and reverse discrimination. In this tape, a panel comprised of well-known judges, government officials, political science scholars and journalists, are debating a hypothetical case of tenure decision. In this case, three professors—one white male, one white female and one black male—are up for tenure decision and only one slot is available; each professor is ranked differently in scholarship, teaching, college services, and so on. No one is rated the best in all the major categories.

Here is how the assignment, titled "Who Would You Recommend for Tenure?" begins:

You have all watched the tape and you all know what is being debated and what is at stake here.

Now assume the role of a tenure committee member at Dolton University (Congratulations! Only tenured professors can savor this kind of power!). Discuss and justify why out of the three candidates you have decided to recommend Professor Goodman (the white female) or Nelson (the white male) or Raspberry (the black male) for tenure (Well, it is a tough job, too!).

A few important things to consider:

You need to pursue your argument with a full awareness of the debate on "affirmative action" that has been going on in this country, especially in the context of higher education. However, this is not to be a broad-stroke discussion about affirmative action. You are working on a specific case involving flesh and blood individuals. How would you blend the general (philosophical and political) and the specific (this particular case) into one coherent and cogent argument?

You need to establish clearly the criteria you are using to make the decision: How much weight should scholarship, teaching, college services, etc. be given respectively? Why? How is each candidate rated against the criteria?

You need to anticipate and address the potential different/opposing recommendations from the other committee members, with a clear purpose of convincing them so as to reach any possible agreement.

Yes, the task is not a light one because the two professors who are denied tenure will have to pack up and find another place to work (if they are that lucky in today's tight job market).

Of course, there are other detailed requirements concerning unity, coherence, emphasis, development and clarity.

At the end of the assignment, five or six students would be selected to form their own panel. They would read their papers to the class, and a heated discussion and debate would follow.

A Dark-haired, Yellow-Faced English Professor

Usually students would vote according to their own race and gender, though a few did cross their respective color line. Regardless of how they voted, they did have a chance to explore the complexities of the issue.

Whenever students asked me how I would vote at such junctures when ideas and values began to clash, however, I'd dodge and hide behind the role I had assumed as the facilitator in the classroom. I wanted to pretend that this affirmative action debate did not affect me at all. Somehow, I was above and beyond all this hoopla. I'd like to believe that I was hired because of my qualifications: my doctoral degree, my teaching experience, and my publishing record.

However, I wasn't 100% sure. I knew that the college's ad in the *Chronicle of Higher Education* included a statement somewhere along the line of "Such and Such College is an AA employer and women and minorities are encouraged to apply." Was I a beneficiary of the much-disputed affirmative action? Was I hired to fill a quotas because I am Chinese?

I did not want to know and I still do not want to know now. I may be a minority in this country demographically and politically, but I do not want to feel so psychologically. That's perhaps why during the last six years of my full-time teaching, I have never attended even one meeting of the college's minority caucus despite numerous messages they have left for me, and despite the fact that I am very sympathetic to their causes.

When I came to this college for my job interview, the Search Committee—five English professors—and I had such a good time talking about issues concerning Academia in general, teaching English more specifically, as well as my credentials. It did not take them long to decide. These five professors and indeed almost all the other professors in the English department have since treated me as one of them rather than an outsider. Through teaching, research, and services, I have made my contributions and earned my place in the college.

In the first couple of years, though, I did occasionally hear some members of the college—from disciplines other than my own—mumbling about "foreigners" being hired. I would bristle. Sometimes, I wanted to confront them and challenge them to an academic duel. Then, I would tell myself: "What the heck! Why should I lose my equilibrium over this? It is not worth it. Just do my work and wait and see if they will shut up." Strange enough, I have not heard any such complaints for quite a while now. Either I have proved myself or they have resigned to a situation they can not do anything about—or a combination of both.

Is there any benefit to having a non-native speaker teaching college English? Because of the 30-plus years I lived in a very different culture, and because of the years I have lived in this culture, I think I have gained some perspectives on subjects ranging from everyday life to academics and politics: food, housing, transportation, democracy, justice, prison labor, human rights, family planning, gun control, environment, etc. In teaching Victorian literature, for example, I try to bring some interesting cross-cultural twists into the class discussion of chastity and fallen woman. The students seem to welcome such perspectives, but is it really beneficial? I have my doubts, sometimes.

In a short story course I was teaching one semester, I included Lu Xun's "A Madman's Diary" to test the taste buds of my students. In this story, written by one of the greatest modern Chinese writers, the protagonist struggles with an agonizing delusion that everybody around him, including his own elder brother, is plotting to murder and eat him. In fact, the story has quite a few allusions to instances of cannibalism in Chinese history: starved residents in a besieged city exchanging their sons to eat, a lowly man cooking his own son as a rare dish to please the curious taste buds of his king, and a dutiful son cutting off a piece of his own flesh and boiling it for his parents to eat in time of famine.

Some of the students were so disgusted by such cannibalistic references in the story, that class discussion could not go on, and important issues—e.g., social and historical themes of the story—were left unexplored. I have never dared to bring this story into any of my literature classes again.

My presence in the college does have some impact on two specific groups: 1) students whose families have immigrated to this country recently, and 2) international students from Japan, South Korea, Pakistan, Uganda, etc. I have a lot in common with them, and I can sympathize with them. I have a good idea about their needs and the challenges facing them. I can give them help which they may not be able to get from professors who have never personally experienced the difficulties of trying to make it in another country. This does not mean that full-blooded American students do not come to my office, or that I do not enjoy talking to them.

In fact, some of them like to sit in my office and have long discussions on hot-button issues of the day. Some are perfectly comfortable talking about absolutely nothing particularly. Still, I feel that there is a unique understanding and bond between myself and my minority and international students. One of the things I relish most is the degree of academic freedom a college professor enjoys. As long as you follow the general guidelines, you are free to teach your classes in any idiosyncratic way, or with any innovative approach you happen to prefer. The students, on their part, enjoy a lot of freedom, too: they are free to choose and change their major, take as many or as few classes as they want to, and they are free to express their own feelings and thoughts, however unpopular these feelings and thoughts might be. In fact, while the professor is busy lecturing, they can lounge in their seats, stretch their legs as far forward as they are able, sip their coffee or soda, munch potato chips and chew gum of all different colors.

Finding it rather annoying and distracting, I have recently taken the liberty to curtail such freedom by banning the munching and chewing act in my classroom. Still, this type of freedom was not available at all when I was a college student in China.

In my writing classes, I normally let my students choose their own topics for papers. I do not believe in forcing students to write on subjects about which they do not care, or only feel a lukewarm interest. Besides, I believe that college education should promote the free exchange of ideas and encourage students to search for truths on their own. This approach, however, can prove challenging to the professor's comfort level.

The first semester I taught as an assistant, a female student—about 18 years old—wrote a paper about contraceptives, and how to use them effectively. She discussed each method: male and female condoms, the diaphragm, the cervical cap, spermicides, pills and withdrawal. Her paper went into such great detail, and described each with such expertise that I blushed profusely as I read the paper.

I had been married and my son was already 6-year-old, but I felt uncomfortable reading such papers, especially written by such a young girl. I had not expected all the female college students in the U.S. to be shy virgins, but I felt like her paper crossed the line. Now, however, I can not only provide meaningful comments in the margins of such papers, but also discuss topics on sexuality in class without blushing at all. I have certainly become more mellow.

Occasionally, though, letting students choose their own topics has had a far more profound effect than simply making me blush. One semester a couple of years ago, I told the students in a class that for their second paper they could write about "anything under the sun," as long as it was a narrative about some unusual personal experience. One student, whose rough draft I had not seen because he did not come for individual conferencing, turned in a paper that was indeed quite unusual.

The paper began as the writer (The "I" in the story) went into a bar and flirted with a blond bar attendant. About half way into the paper, the two ended up in bed. From there on it was out-and-out hardcore porn.

I knew I was in trouble. If I rejected the paper, I would be called on it because of the "anything under the sun" clause I had promised, and more importantly because of First Amendment protection. If I accepted the paper, I would be put in a compromising position as if I endorsed such trash as academic. In addition, I suspected that the paper could have been downloaded from some dubious website because its prose sophistication was well above that of the student writer, and because I knew for a fact that he was spending a lot of time in chat rooms and the dimly-lit corners of cyberspace. So I gambled.

I returned his paper with this end comment: I do not feel comfortable grading this paper because of the subject matter. I suggest that you cut the second part of the paper and expand on the first and explore more thoroughly the significance of the encounter. As expected, the student did not take this well.

From then on, he became more disruptive in the classroom. Whenever I gave a new assignment, he would mumble something about my not keeping my word, and would not stop when I told him to. At last, I lost it and said to him very sternly, in front of the whole class: "If I ever come across a book with some macho guy and chick on the glossy cover, and it has your name as author, I will never let anyone know that you were once a student in my writing class!" That shut him up. He actually became more cooperative in class from then on. And from then on, I have never dared to include the "anything under the sun" grand gesture in my assignments.

Even though my suspicion of plagiarism concerning the porn paper was never corroborated by evidence, the next one was an open-and-shut case. Unhappy with the low grades he had received on his first two papers, this student—who had

A Dark-haired, Yellow-Faced English Professor 63

been struggling with some basics—surprised me with his third paper. Its perceptiveness, lucidity and eloquence almost reached the level of Roger Rosenblatt, Charles Krauthammer or Calvin Trillin, some of my favorite *Time* writers. For a brief time, I was rather impressed with how I had whipped this mediocre writer into shape. I almost wished that Mr. Alfred Nobel had included teaching as a category in the annual awards named after him. I knew that while miracles such as this do happen in life, my teaching may not have been the catalyst in this particular case. So I invited the student to my office, sat him down and began to chat with him.

"I enjoyed reading your essay very much. But before I go any further in praising it, I have to ask you: did you write it yourself, or did you have help?" I began.

"I wrote it." he answered confidently.

"Indeed. Now, I particularly like your intro paragraph. It grabs my attention right away. I'll tell you what, here is a sheet of paper. Can you recall what you put in the intro?"

"I wrote it days ago. How would I remember?" He looked hurt.

From a shelf on my bookcase, I found a published essay of mine and pushed it over to him. "I can't say I'll be able to recall the whole thing verbatim, but I shouldn't be too far off."

Still mumbling, he agreed to give it a try.

After struggling for a few minutes, he was done. The fruit of his labor, however, didn't look anything like the intro in the paper at all, in subject matter or in sentence sophistication. But he still insisted that he was the sole and only author of that paper. I could not help but play my trump card. Pointing to a parenthetical instruction in the paper, to wit, (see photo), I asked: "Where's the photo, Mister?"

Such direct confrontations sometimes meant trouble, though. At least one time, I felt my safety was at stake. At the time, I was still a graduate teaching assistant. This student came to class in the first week, then disappeared altogether, until the last week of the semester. He showed up, put a pile of things he had written on my desk, and asked me to pass him. It took me a second or two to even recall who he was.

"I'm sorry, but I thought you'd dropped the class. Where have you been all these months?" I asked.

"Oh, I went on a bunch of hunting trips," he replied, with a smile on his face.

It turned out that he had called up someone in the class, and found out about the assignments. So he had all the work done. I told him that I could not accept his work because of the university's attendance policy, etc.

Unwilling to give up, he challenged me to prove his absences. I had the tangible evidence of the roster and all the other students in the class as eyewitnesses. And the pile of writings he had just turned in. Standing up—a rather tall and husky fellow—to leave, he threatened: "Just you wait. You'll be hearing from my lawyer!"

Oh, my! I was somewhat shaken. Going over some of his writings, out of curiosity, I was gripped by this fact: he was an avid hunter, and he had an impressive collection of automatics and semiautomatics. I was scared: "What if?" The tragedy of a disgruntled Chinese student on a shooting spree in Iowa City was still fresh in my mind. So I went to my graduate director, Dr. Woodson.

"Don't you worry," he reassured me, his eyes showing the same warmth, curiosity, care and sarcasm that he had shown on many other occasions. His thumbs still twiddled ceaselessly. "We'll get you a much bigger lawyer if he sues. But it won't do you any harm to be a little bit more careful."

I went back and waited for my phone to ring, or to see anything suspicious in my mailbox. I never heard from that student's lawyer. In fact, the next semester, I saw him tramping in and out of a classroom next to the class I was teaching, burdened by a heavy school bag on his back. He had bluffed and I hadn't budged. It was over.

The linguistics scholars I mentioned earlier may be onto something when they expound on the deterioration of one's talent for language acquisition at the onset of puberty, at least in the aspect of speaking a new language. While my spoken English is fluent enough with a mixture of British and American accents, my mother tongue—Chinese—likes to reassert itself now and then.

Once or twice in a semester, while lecturing, I catch myself off guard with a word or two in Chinese. Interestingly enough, nobody in the class has ever mentioned, or even seems to have noticed these linguistic blunders. Maybe they think I am saying something so profound that they had failed to understand and are afraid of embarrassing themselves by asking me what I mean.

A Dark-haired, Yellow-Faced English Professor

In addition to teaching, I have been writing, too. Not too long ago, at a panel discussion of a writers' conference sponsored by my college, a student who had published some writings of her own asked me, "Why don't I feel like a writer yet?" I replied that I don't feel I am a writer either, though I have published a thing or two. Why? Because in Chinese, "writer" is usually translated as *zuojia*, which means "master writer." "Master" anything would be too heavy a title for my head. In English, however, and in theory, we are all writers. My response to that student may reflect my split identity as a Chinese English professor.

As an aside, the Chinese equivalent for "professor" is *jiaoshou*. It carries the same connotation of erudition and respect as in English. I hope that one day when I introduce myself as such, I won't perceive a reaction that hovers somewhere between surprise and doubt. For now, foreign-born professors of English are not a rare species in the U.S.

A Letter in Spring

MARCH, 1996

Dear Dad:

It's already Spring.

Outside the window, dry and tawny lawns are turning green; in front of the house, burgeoning daffodils, tulips and other flowers are gently prodding open the top layer of soft soil, and will soon be budding and blossoming; tender leaves are quietly shooting forth from the twigs of the American basswood you planted behind our house; and birds are chirping and twittering in the ironwood trees in the woods not very far from here.

When you receive this letter, Spring will be in full bloom everywhere!

But in my heart, there is not an inkling of Spring. In my heart, it is still Winter, bitter, icy cold Winter. It all started that night, early last June.

I was deep in sleep. Whether I heard the persistent ringing in a dream, or was awakened by it, I am not sure now. I picked up the phone and heard my brother on the other side of the Pacific. He told me—in a shaken voice—to be prepared for bad news: You had just been diagnosed with lung cancer; it was already at an advanced stage; and the prognosis was not very good. I felt cold, as if a bucketful of icy water had been poured over my head on a freezing cold, winter day. I was shivering all over uncontrollably.

Was this a dream? A bad dream? When I woke up in the morning, would I be able to shake my head and say, "Oh, what a dream!" and all would be okay?

If it was indeed a bad dream, there was no waking up in the next few months and in the many more days and months to follow.

Ever since then and ever since you left us on the early morning of October 5th, last year, this world has lost its light, its color, its warmth and its music.

Everyday, when I wake up early in the morning, drive to work, sit at the table to eat my meals, or toss and turn in bed on another sleepless night, I can hear a deep and plaintive voice resounding in my heart:
Dad is gone.

My heart is seized with a gnawing pain; I am lost in a bottomless melancholy; and I cry over and over again, silently:
This is not true! This is only a dream! Dad will come back again!

Numerous times, you did come back! Numerous times, I did see you again!

In dreams.

A flickering oil-lamp in a little clay house. A baby boy was being born into a family already too large and too poor to welcome this extra mouth, crying for food. Somebody suggested pouring a bowlful of water on his face, but his mother protested and he was let to live.

A toddler walking unsteadily on a narrow, uneven ridge in the rice fields suddenly lost balance and fell into a little pond of muddy water. He kicked his little legs, splashed his small hands and swallowed many mouthfuls, but somehow he got himself out of the pond and survived.

A lad, bashful but proud, was marching through a cheering crowds of teachers, pupils, and villagers gathered at the school's entrance to welcome the first prize winner of a district-wide composition contest. Firecrackers sparked in the air. The essay he wrote was about a dream in which he was fighting a hungry tiger that had attacked him and his little brother. He had won the battle, of course.

A high school student, full of promise, had just been told bluntly by a doctor that he suffered from tuberculosis, a near incurable condition at that time. Henceforth, he would be denied many opportunities to advance in his education and his career: "Do I still have a future?" he would ask himself, in despair.

Undaunted, this young man turned his gaze toward the yellow earth and green fields of his ancestors, and threw himself into the cause of building a new socialist motherland. There, he sought and found the meaning of his life, and was decorated with gold medals for his sweat and toil and sacrifices.

Overworked, he succumbed to another fit of tuberculosis, coughing up blood in the middle of night, with death hovering above him. But he recovered, after a long fight. Again, he won the battle.

A Letter in Spring

With famine still raging all over the country during the so-called "Three Years of Disasters," he turned his talent and energies to providing educational opportunities to the kids of poor and disadvantaged peasants. He built a middle school, using clay houses and make-do wooden tables and stools. He wrote and compiled the school's own textbooks, taught classes and plowed the fields so that his teachers and students would not starve or die of hunger.

A 30-plus-year-old middle school principal—a tall cone-shaped hat on his head and his body wrapped in inky "big character" posters—was being pushed roughly by a gang of Red Guards along a little twisting road on the warm soil to which he had vowed to devote his whole life. Beating a cracked gong, he was trudging forward with difficulty while shouting slogans to "down with" himself.

He was being confined in a small, dark room of a dilapidated building in the back of a weed-plagued schoolyard. His 10-year-old second son came to visit him with a dish made of vegetables and shrimp that he had caught himself with a small basket. His son had seen through window panes how brutally his beloved Father had been struggled with, had been forced to kneel down on broken glass, and had had to bend low with a heavy blackboard hanging on his neck on thin wire. His son cried at the sight of reddish bruises on his father's body, but Father told him that he was confident that one day he would be "emancipated" by the people.

When "the Cultural Revolution" was over, he revived and rededicated himself to the education of the kids of the poor and disadvantaged peasants, with even more enthusiasm and vigor, as if caught in a race against time. He would leave home very early in the morning, and would not return until supper had been cold for a long time. During those days and nights, the ringing of his bicycle bell at the door was the most musical of all sound to his family: Dad is back!

Dad, I have seen you in my dreams so many times. But my memory about the years since I—your second son—went to college in 1977 is blurry. Since then, I have been drifting like a homeless cloud, from place to place, and from one side of the Pacific to the other. Nevertheless, your letters have always followed me wherever I happened to be. Every few weeks, for the last 17-plus years, I would open the mailbox and find a letter from you with your neat and familiar handwriting on the cover, and I'd run back to my dorm or basement room I was sharing with others, open it up, and read it several times.

My memory about the last couple of years is much clearer. At JFK International Airport, you, gray-haired, not having seen us for six years and having finally retired, rushed towards us, your grandson greeting you and mother with fresh, blooming flowers. We got to spend the longest and "happiest" (in your own words) time together ever since I left home for college.

Together, we played chess and cards, talked about our family, our motherland, the whole world and the future.

We went picnicking and shopping, visited schools and played dinner guest at friends' homes.

We installed the carpet in the basement of our newly-bought house, painted the stairway leading to the basement, assembled a multifunctional home gym, and planted flowers and trees in our garden.

We celebrated Thanksgiving, Christmas, New Year's Eve, Chinese New Year, and your birthday.

We visited the Empire State Building, the World Trade Center, the United Nations, the Statue of Liberty, Ellis Island, Independence Hall, Gettysburg, and the City Island on the Susquehanna River.

And you read tales and tales from the *Warring States* and the *Water-Margin* and other Chinese classics to your grandson, and taught him Chinese. You wrote all the time, recording your feelings and thoughts during your visit.

Those were days of happiness! And I still have on videotape the last chess game you played with your grandson; you two stopped in the middle of the game, leaving it for your next visit to finish it off.

I should not have consented to your going back in the still chilly, early Spring. Otherwise, you might not have caught that cold which eventually led to the terminal diagnosis, but you missed home so much!

I can never forgive myself. I went back only once and stayed by your bedside for only two weeks when you were fighting for your very life. And above all I did not go back to bid you farewell for the last time when you left us forever.

When you—lying on a simple bed—saw me walking into the room you were sharing with two other very ill patients, tears flowed down your cheeks and you choked up with emotions. I picked up a tissue to dry your eyes while trying in vain to hold

A Letter in Spring

back my own. Two weeks later, when it was time for me to leave, I did not have the courage to go to your room and look at you one more time—even though it might be the last time.

Then, every time I called, the news was worse. You were still fighting, but your condition was deteriorating fast. You were in constant pain, excruciating and dehumanizing pain. I—thousands of miles away—could do nothing but pray in my heart that a miracle would happen. You—of all the people I have known—deserved it.

Miracles didn't happen. You left us on that early morning in October. I wasn't there.

I knew—and know—that I had no right to be angry with anyone even though my prayer had not been answered. Perhaps millions of people in similar situations have also prayed and their prayers have not been answered either.

Would it have made a difference had I been more receptive to those good-hearted and well-intentioned people who had shown their concern for my soul and spiritual being? Oh, they have tried so many times. On many a quiet night, I had wandered on my own in the Garden, listened to the Sermons on the Mount, and followed Noah on the ark. I was moved, but I was not moved enough to open up my heart. I was a hardened agnostic. Perhaps my non-belief was due to the way I was brought up, the things I had been through, the books I had read, and the thoughts I had thought.

Maybe, I should have been more receptive. Would that have made a difference? Grandpa—your father—was a pious, Buddhist believer: kind-hearted, loving, soft-spoken, patient, hardworking and a vegetarian. He had never hurt anyone, not a single living thing. Moreover, he prayed, and I can still see him vividly in my mind's eye, squatting on a straw mat in front of a small statue of Buddha, meditating or murmuring scriptures for hours, his hands shakily turning a rosary. Despite his piety, he lost his first wife and several of his young sons and daughters to either illness, poverty, or a combination of both.

And I believed—and still believe—that you don't have to be a believer in order to be a good man, to be kind and useful to your fellow human beings.

Yet, sometimes, I have my doubts. Perhaps, perhaps, it could have made a difference if I had prayed as a believer. Perhaps I would still be able to open the mail box and find a letter inside from you with your familiar, neat handwriting on the cover; I would again hear the ringing of the bicycle bell at the door of my childhood home, and you could come and visit us again to finish off that unfinished chess game with your grandson.

All I have now are the memories, your letters and your memoirs—*Sixty Springs and Autumns*—which I edited with tears in my eyes while you were still in the hospital. I had it printed and professionally bound. The only comforting thought is that you had a chance to listen to the first few edited pages and nod your approval.

Dad, the grass is greening, the trees are alive with new leaves, the flowers are blossoming and the birds are singing.

Please accept these Spring colors, Spring flowers, and Spring melodies as greetings from the heart of a wandering son from afar!

With love,
Shouhua

The In-laws Are Coming!

IT WAS A SUNNY, BREEZY MORNING in May of 1998. I was driving 70 miles an hour on Interstate 78, leaving fleeting behind me the sometimes flat, sometimes hilly, green farmland of the Pennsylvania Dutch, as if I was in the middle of a 3D movie. My destination was John F. Kennedy International Airport in New York. My wife was sitting next to me in the passenger seat. My occasional peripheral glance caught her sniffling and applying one tissue after another to her nose and eyes. Things were not so good. This was unusual for May.

May is usually one of the sunniest and most happy months for our family. May 1st, is our only son's birthday; the 10th is Mother's Day which, as in most families, is celebrated much more seriously than Father's Day in the following month. The 17th is my wife's birthday. You know what that means. And then there is *Duanwujie*, the Dragon Boat Festival, that wraps up the month of festivities.

Besides, whenever just the two of us drive anywhere—which does not happen too often any more—we like to tease each other a bit. The usual kind of sweet nonsense that is exchanged between a couple who find themselves in a common situation. The reminiscing about all of our first-times, coaxed out of each other, one by one, as a sort of renewal of our marriage vows. Little sparks start to fly as eager hands play and search out each other's warm grip. It works to rekindle—at least for the moment—the fire of romance that gets dimmed by everyday routines.

But now she sat next to me, sullen, sniffling, and making frequent use of the tissue box.

Her parents—my in-laws—were coming to visit us all the way from China, across thousands of miles and almost a dozen time zones. We were supposed to be happy, to be excited, to be singing our hearts out as we raced across the Interstate to the airport. This is what any good Chinese children who were properly brought up should do.

I still recall that September afternoon in 1994, when we—my wife, our son, and myself—were sailing on the same Interstate to New York to meet my parents who were coming to visit us. We hadn't seen them for more than six years. By that September, I had already survived the purgatory of a doctoral program, and had been teaching in a college as a professor for a year, driving to work every day listening to "Fresh Air" and "All Things Considered" on NPR.

We had already moved into our first house, a little two-story contemporary thing built from the ground up in a nice, new suburban development. The rich colors of the Blue Mountains spread out in the background. My wife had just started working in a pathology lab at a medical college not far from home, having had to commute every other week for over six months between her job in the Bronx, New York, and our home in Harrisburg. Our son was doing great in school. We were just beginning to live the American dream, every facet of it.

So what was wrong today?

Because so much has happened between then and now. In the past four years, I lost my dear father to lung cancer. That was in 1995. Then, about a year later, my wife lost her mother—her biological mother—to complications from heart surgery. She was the most soft-spoken, tender hearted soul I have ever known.

What lingers in my mind the most, even today, is the last glance I had of her in the summer of 1996. We were getting ready to board the train on the first leg of our long trip back to the U.S. All of our friends and relatives were on the railway platform, bidding us farewell. At the spur of the moment, I ran back to the van parked outside the station to check if we had left anything in it. In the van I found my mother-in-law, small, all alone, sitting in a back seat, her head bending very low, and tears washing down her reddened cheeks. She did not have the strength to come to the platform to say goodbye to her daughter, her favorite grandchild, and me.

So, we could not be cheerful that sunny, breezy morning in May. Actually, we had a challenge in front of us: what term of address should we use to greet my wife's new stepmother? We had already racked our brains over this many times before, to no avail, as if this formality meant the whole world to us.

As any good Chinese son-in-law or daughter-in-law knows, you should always address your spouse's parents as "Father" or "Mother." In China, of all countries in the world, there has been a dramatic increase—in the last ten years or so—of marriages or remarriages of elderly people who have lost their lifetime spouses. Many a widow and widower are eager to start again, and find a companion with whom to sit and watch the sun set in its last glories.

While this development gives them a second chance to pursue happiness, it also brings with it some problems, not the least of which are the terms of address. American culture can handle this transition without much fanfare by staying on a first name basis until a bond develops that warrants the use of "Mom" or "Dad," Chinese culture expects the new members to bond with each other right away.

In Chinese culture, which emphasizes propriety and respect to the elderly, you are expected to address everyone—relative or stranger—of your parents' generation as "Uncle" or "Aunt." The new spouse of your father or mother (or father-in-law or mother-in-law) deserves nothing less. That is exactly what most Chinese people that I know, do in such situations: they call that special new member of their family "Uncle" or "Aunt," or resort to the "Last Name + Uncle or Aunt" formula.

We wouldn't have needed to rack our brains over this had my wife's new stepmother not insisted in a letter to us, prior to her marriage to my father-in-law, that her consent to marry him was contingent upon her being respected and loved exactly as a biological mother. We knew that calling her anything other than "mother" would not be respecting and loving her as our own dear mother. But calling a sixty-year-old stranger who was now suddenly, by law and through unhappy circumstances, a member of your family—"mother," would not be easy.

"Mother" is a term of address that should be reserved exclusively for that one individual in the whole universe in whose womb you started your life, with whom you were once connected through an umbilical cord: for the one who fed you, nursed you, washed your diapers, taught your first words, cheered for you, worried for you, screamed at you many times and spanked your butt when you misbehaved stupidly. "Mother" was the one whose heart you have broken at least once, and who shed hot tears when you were boarding the train or airplane to seek adventures in another country thousands of miles away. Of course, by virtue of your union with your spouse, his or her mother is entitled to that endearing term, too.

But a strange, old woman?

She had not existed as far as we were concerned before the marriage. She had existed only as an abstraction up until that morning in May. She had married my father-in-law before the one-year anniversary of my real mother-in-law's death. Before the marriage became a fact, I had timidly murmured my concerns. I felt it was too soon.

I felt that he should wait until we had come to terms with the loss, and until we were emotionally more or less ready to accept a substitute. But I was only a son-in-law. As the only person who has earned an advanced degree from an American university, I was supposed to be the enlightened one of the family. Besides, in a China as open as it is today, dating too long, or shacking up without tying the knot in due time would still be frowned upon. Most importantly, my father-in-law was feeling lonely, and life without a companion was proving very hard for a 70-year-old.

His youngest daughter—my wife—was an ocean away. His son and two other daughters—all married with children, live in another faraway, vibrant city called Shengzhen, right across from Hong Kong. I could see how loneliness would be a problem for him.

AS WE WERE WAITING at the terminal for international flights at JFK, we were still nowhere near a solution. We were about to give up, and to simply switch off our hearts for the split second when we had to utter that most endearing term in the world to a stranger.

Suddenly, we spotted a familiar face in the stream of faces flowing out of the terminal. Then, our searching eyes caught sight of another face right next to the familiar one. Apparition-like. The most anxiously waited for face in the whole world at that moment. Just then, my wife said, as if hit by something, "How about calling her Han Mama?"

"Great!" I snapped back, as if I was being sucked into a violent crosscurrent. I would have grabbed at just about anything.

"Han Mama" has all the dearness of "mother" in it, yet with her last name added, she is unequivocally separated from my wife's own mother and my real mother-in-law. In fact, in Chinese culture, it is proper to address a woman of your mother's generation respectfully by using the "Last Name + Mama" formula. Thus, "Han Mama" is mother—and is not mother. What an outburst of creativity under extreme pressure!

The In-Laws are Coming!

Life seemed to relax almost immediately.

In the flurry of excitement—presenting flowers, handshaking, hugging, taking pictures for remembrance's sake and checking luggage, plus all the incoherent questions and answers about the trip, there was no way that I could have gauged how Han Mama registered her new title.

So much for all the brain cells that had been lost over this. Now she became real. She was with us. Han Mama looked her age: medium height for a Chinese woman, gray hair combed back neatly and tied into a nice knot, and her face benefiting from a hint of makeup. Her eyes radiated vibrantly. Buoyed by whatever vigor was left in her thin body after such a journey, she was amiable, talking to us as if we had known each other for so many years. Father-in-law, his hair now completely grayed, was all smiles, too. He was in very good spirits. Everybody seemed very happy.

My in-laws were visiting us. They were going to stay with us for the next several months. Three? Four? Five? Six? We didn't know yet.

HAN MAMA PROVED a very likeable person. In fact, she and my wife hit it off right from the start. Having made a quick guided tour of our house, admired and then offered some tips on improving our home's interior, Han Mama quickly found her way to the kitchen, joining my wife there to prepare our first meal together.

Soon, the kitchen was throbbing with life: knives galloping down chopping boards, vegetables splashing in the sink, the sound of woks, pans, and ladles of different sizes tolling like bells, fresh, jumbo shrimps sizzling in hot oil, and black mushrooms, dried bamboo shoots, and other unknown ingredients bubbling in rich broth. A strange delicious aroma was expanding into every corner of the house.

On top of this symphonic and olfactory event, Han Mama talked excitedly about her life, her kids, her grandkids, her students, her colleagues, and so on and so forth. By the time we sat down, she had almost introduced them all into our world. My wife filled her in about her father, his habits, temper, likes and dislikes, as if Han Mama—his newly wedded wife—hadn't already discovered these on her own.

The dinner on the table that evening tasted different from the delicacies my wife usually prepared for us. My taste buds were confused at first, then teased a little bit. Finally, they adjusted and welcomed the change. My wife was quick to point out what she liked the most.

Proud and happy, Father-in-law had a very good appetite. He had had enough of the food on airplanes. My son, however, who was allergic to seafood and never had much interest in things like black mushrooms or bamboo shoots anyway, found the change overwhelming. He swallowed his food one small spoonful at a time, very quietly.

Apparently, Han Mama had one thing in common with my wife: a passion for the kitchen. From that first day forward, I would often find them in the kitchen, engrossed in the sharing of secrets, mostly on the art of food making.

Soon, Han Mama took over the kitchen, a place where my wife had prepared so many delicious dinners and played hostess to so many dear friends. With my wife's own mother in all those fifteen years I had known them, the takeover had always been the other way round. Whenever she went back to her mother's, my wife would play chef in the kitchen (I would be content with the role of the chef's assistant and dishwasher). Her mother had trained all three daughters in the intricate art of food making when they were very young.

Her father was a lifetime food connoisseur of sorts. Every time he returned home from some dinner or banquet, he would try to recall the flavor and ingredients in a certain dish that he had particularly enjoyed. Then his daughters, with the directions of their mother, would pick up the cues, and plunge into a full-scale, culinary adventure in the kitchen until they emerged with something their father finally approved of. All those years of apprenticeship had not gone for nothing: the three sisters had acquired quite a reputation among the family's friends and relatives for the excellent dishes they could prepare.

Han Mama's passion for cooking was a much more recent development. Her interest was not only in the flavor, but also in the nutritional and medicinal benefits. "Dried bamboo shoots have a lot of fiber and thus increase bowel movement . . . and help clean up the whole excretory system," she would comment knowledgeably at the dinner table. "Dark green vegetables are rich in Vitamins A, B, C. . . which help prevent cancerous cells from developing and spreading. . . " We would listen respectfully, nod in agreement and try to enjoy the food all the more with the newly gained perspective. Soon, she began

The In-Laws are Coming!

to tell me—the family's professional dishwasher—where to put what utensils according to her new configurations for the kitchen. My wife was happy at first. Now she did not have to hurry back from her eight-to-five job, and cook dinner everyday for a much bigger family. However, gradually, I could sense an unspoken resentment on her part. As if her role as hostess of the household was being usurped. She was also concerned about the reduced appetite in our son.

At any rate, she began to try to regain a bit of control in the kitchen. Now and then, she would cook a favorite dish for her father—*tan chu yu* (a kind of fish dish prepared with sweet and sour sauce), for example, which would taste so fresh, so tender and so delicious. Father-in-law would savor every bit of it. "Excellent! Excellent!" he'd exclaim as his chopsticks picked up another piece from the plate, "This is what I call a fish dish! This is what I have missed!" Han Mama would smile enthusiastically, nod in agreement, but did I detect an uneasiness in her smile?

Soon, every day before leaving for work, my wife would leave a list of the dishes to be prepared for dinner that day. That list would include something special for her father, something special for her stepmother and something special for our son. As to herself and me, we would be happy if everybody else was happy. With the new arrangement, our son's appetite came back, but I'm not so sure of Han Mama whose newly acquired authority in the kitchen had been comprehensively curtailed.

As host and hostess, my wife and I felt obligated to introduce our guests to some authentic American food. Of course, McDonald's, KFC, Pizza Hut and other American fast food restaurants had already become household names in the cosmopolitan areas along the east coast of China. They had excited the taste buds of many Chinese, particularly the young.

Whether out of curiosity or craving for things new and foreign, young Chinese seem to love American fast food. In my hometown Nanjing alone, there are at least half a dozen KFC's, even in places once regarded as havens of traditional Chinese culture such as *Fuzimiao*, the Confucian Temple.

At any rate, we took our guests to Old Country Buffet for dinner, Burger King for lunch and we ordered pizza carryout once. But they didn't like any of it.

Father-in-law's stomach would not accept chicken or fish sandwiches, French fries, or iced soda. Every time, he would pay dearly for his foreign cuisine adventure; he would cough and throw up all he had eaten and his mouth would go bitter from bile. He'd need cup after cup of hot green tea freshly made to restore peace in his stomach. He'd vow that he'd rather have *Yanzhunmian*, plain noodles, with nothing fancy added, than try burgers and sandwiches again.

At Old Country Buffet, Han Mama couldn't find anything she really liked other than ice cream. We quickly abandoned such adventures and turned to the old, beaten track: Chinese restaurants and buffets. Here they would feel most at home, and could eat to their hearts' content.

Han Mama and I had something in common, too. A graduate of a prestigious university in Beijing, she is a retired *te ji jiao shi*, a sort of Distinguished Teacher, the highest honor bestowed on an elementary or secondary school teacher for exceptional achievements. Soon after their arrival, Father-in-law proudly announced to me, "Xiao Hua, you know what, your Han Mama (he had been rather quick in picking up the new title we had invented for her) is *tao li man tian xia!*" Literally translated, her peaches and plums are everywhere under the skies, which figuratively means students she has taught are all over the world.

She majored in Chinese while in college, and I had read quite a bit on my own in classic and contemporary Chinese literature. To prove myself a worthy stepson-in-law, I found all my published writings in Chinese and gave them to her to read: personal essays, literary critiques, short stories as well as translations. She was interested, and took time to read them all. When she was done, she announced that they were not bad. In fact, she even caught a few punctuation errors here and there, which I quickly brushed off and blamed on careless typesetters and editors.

I taught two sessions that summer. I had a 8:00–11:30 schedule, Monday through Thursday. During the weekdays, I would be done by noon and would come back and join the in-laws and my son for lunch. After lunch, I'd pick up where I had left the day before in a book I was working on. They'd retire to the guestroom for their nap. When they got up from a 2-hour long nap, they'd turn on the TV in the family room downstairs and watch whatever was on CCTV (Central China TV): news, panel discussions, or a TV drama series.

The In-Laws are Coming! 81

We could access CCTV programs through a receiver and a satellite dish without paying a monthly subscription fee. My little office was on the second floor. Since the wall facing the open stairway is only about four feet high, I became an uninvited audience for whatever they were watching at the moment. Of course, the in-laws were very thoughtful. They kept the volume rather low, but the sound was still loud enough to find its way into my office.

One afternoon, as I was searching for not-so-nonsensical things to type into the computer, I was also listening to the muddy and violent waters, pounding on the weakened dikes of the Yangze, Songhua, and other rivers and lakes in China, and to President Jiang's loud and spirited pep talks as he visited the flood-fighting heroes on the front.

I came down from the "ivory tower" and joined my in-laws, the soldiers and thousands of peasants in their epic struggle against nature spinning out of control. The sublime spectacle of young soldiers and peasants using their bare-backed bodies as barricades between the beastly flood and millions of innocent people, was indeed moving.

Afterwards, I went upstairs again to try and calm down: to refocus and to get some work done. I had deadlines to meet. But watching TV with the in-laws did have an impact. I wrote a check and sent it to a charity organization in Beijing, and they called Han Mama's son in Nanjing to make a donation of no small sum on their behalf.

Sometimes, while watching the blood-stirring TV coverage, we'd discuss the events. One time, I commented that there was simply too much coverage of Jiang himself. Everyday the first news item was about Jiang and this would last somewhere between five to ten minutes. The focus, I said, should be on the young soldiers and peasants, the common folks, their hardship, their heroism and their sacrifices. My in-laws, however, looked at it from a very different perspective.

In times of such crisis, they lectured, China needed strong, decisive leadership, and Jiang was providing that effectively. But does China need personality cult again? Do the Chinese people want to return to the era of strong man politics? I had my doubts.

Then, the Clintons visited China. They received an imperial welcome in the ancient city of Xian. They climbed the Great Wall in the remote suburbs of Beijing. President Clinton delivered a speech to some six hundred Beijing University students. The in-laws, particularly Han Mama, were glued to the screen.

She admired how young, good looking and energetic Clinton was. She was full of regret that he had stooped so low in an affair with a young woman who was not even pretty by her standards: Monica was too fat. She was baffled that the media would dare to flood the screen with so much embarrassing footage about the president of a country. Father-in-law would shrug his shoulders with a "What's the big deal? What else did you expect in America?" expression on his face.

I would feel called upon to explain the political structure and process in the U.S. as far as I understood it. Is it excessive? Trashy? Humiliating? Destructive? You bet. But it seems an unavoidable price that has to be paid for the choice the founding fathers and the people have made for their country. One would be hard put to imagine anything remotely close to this on Chinese TV, at least not in the foreseeable future.

The U.S. and China seem to represent two extremes. One is shamelessly and almost sadistically exposing and self-exposing to the point that nothing is sacred. The other one is too vulnerable, insecure, and even paranoid, hiding behind masks, layers of impenetrable screens, and smoke-filled rooms. Is there a happy mean somewhere in between?

These on-and-off discussions while watching TV would naturally lead to Tiananmen Square, U.S.-China relations, religion, Taiwan, Hong Kong, democracy and other more sensitive topics. Sometimes our views were not far apart. Sometimes, we were as far apart as the two poles.

One day, one thing led to another and the subject of homosexuality came up. While homosexuality has always existed in China, it is such a taboo subject that it is avoided altogether in public discourse. I announced to them that in Beijing, Shanghai, and perhaps other big cities, gay organizations were now quite active though they still remain underground.

Scandalized, Father-in-law questioned the reliability of my sources: newspapers and magazines published in the U.S. Noticing a sneer on his face, and spurred by a rebellious and heretic impulse at the moment, I declared, "I don't see anything wrong if there are many gays and lesbians in China. Who knows, it may even be a good thing for China. At least it will help relieve the population burden in the long run."

They almost flipped out, staring at me as if I had just parachuted down from the Mars. They remained speechless, their eyes full of hurt and disappointment. I began to question

The In-Laws are Coming! 83

myself. Have I stayed in America too long and been corrupted beyond all hope by its decadent culture? Sometimes when I found it really difficult to concentrate and became genuinely concerned about missing the deadline, I'd resort to a pair of ear plugs my wife had bought me for use in the shower. The plugs, when I inserted them firmly in my ears, did succeed in blocking the TV sound bites from downstairs, but another kind of sound—a constant low-keyed humming—would begin to spiral and fill every brain cell in my skull. Writing became impossible. Luckily, they didn't watch too much TV, so I didn't have to resort to the earplugs often.

After a daily dose of TV, Han Mama would read and write for a while, and work on her English vocabulary. With an English-Chinese dictionary, she translated into Chinese all the items listed in an advertisement of a local grocery store. She'd ask me or her new grandson how to say this or that in English, and what a particular word in English meant in Chinese. Father-in-law had changed a lot, too. He used to be a restless and constantly on-the-go type. Now, he would sit at the dinner table or lie on the couch for hours, going over every single item in the *People's Daily* and the few other Chinese publications we had. He even started to keep a diary, recording every bit of the events in his life during his visit. When all this was done, though, he would be restless, again. He'd play poker by himself or try to solve some puzzles by moving the cards around and arranging them in different patterns.

When they had just arrived, Father-in-law announced to us that his highest objective for this trip was "safety and health." When this was ensured, he added, he would consider some sightseeing and finding out for himself what all the hoopla about America was. With his age and his medical condition—high blood pressure and a pacemaker—this was a wise plan.

Long before their arrival, my wife and I had planned over and again how to make their stay a happy and healthy experience. When we took them to visit Washington DC, New York, Philadelphia, Atlantic City, Gettysburg, etc., we had to make sure he had all his medication and enough boiled water, and that all his other needs were taken care of.

Father-in-law later told us that on our way to the Atlantic City, he had been extremely worried. He had almost asked us to stop and turn back. What he had in his mind were the images of casinos he had got from movies: dimly lit, smoke-filled rooms, gangsters jumping on you from dark corners, masked robbers kicking your door down in the middle of night, and people disappearing mysteriously, bodies being dumped in dark alleys and on and on.

The Caesar's Palace we visited, however, turned out to be clean and well-lit. Everything was going on in an orderly fashion. Rows and rows of slot machines were singing at the same time, inviting and promising to make your dreams come true.

I bought a cupful of coins for him and he began to play. Whenever he put in a few coins and saw many more jingling down, he would be excited and jump like a kid. He would win five, ten or twenty coins after putting one or two, and then lose them all—and more. After the last coin was swallowed up by the greedy machines a few hours later, he could still not tear himself away from them. Later, he said that he would have liked to visit Atlantic City again and again, but seeing that we were very busy, he did not bring it up.

In addition to these longer excursions, we'd try to take them on shorter trips to places close by, at least once a week. We had parties at home, and brought them along to the homes of friends, both Chinese and American.

They had such fun at dance parties organized by local Chinese associations. In fact, Han Mama and Father-in-law became instant stars because they were such avid and graceful dancers. Oh, they could waltz and tango so well, and they knew so many different steps and moves. They were such a charming couple!—everybody who got to know them would tell us.

Every evening, with twilight still lingering over the ridges of the Blue Mountains behind our development, the two would take a little walk, hand in hand. Han Mama was naturally the PR person of the two. She would greet everyone they ran into on the sidewalks with a warm "Hi!" and start a conversation with the few English expressions she had just picked up, using gestures and facial expressions rather creatively. Father-in-law would stand by, smiling and making approving noises in Chinese.

Han Mama even charmed a little, 2-year-old boy called Jon, who lives a few houses down the drive. He took a liking to her right away when they were introduced. Every day, when he spotted her and Father-in-law strolling down the drive, he'd yell out her first name, "Xiang, Xiang! Mom, it's Xiang there!" which means "sweet-smelling" in Chinese.

That affection, of course, was not one-sided. Everyday, when she returned from walking, she'd marvel "Oh, how blue his eyes are!" over and again. One evening, she ran back into the house, grabbed the camera and had photos taken together with her young friend so she could look at that pair of blues again when she returned to China.

All was well except when Han Mama and Father-in-law got into fights. It was never over much of anything, but they would not be on speaking terms with each other for a couple of days. Han Mama's face would cloud over. She would complain of her arthritis. She would make a loud noise which is hard to describe, something between a hiccup and a moan.

We would worry. My wife would have to play marriage counselor by sitting them down and listening to her complaining about how Father-in-law was insensitive, bossy, and clueless as to how to express his love for her in tender language. If the counselor needed any reinforcement, I'd pitch in. A short while after the counseling sessions, the sky would be sunny again, and we could all breathe more easily.

Sure, they would have liked to enlarge the periphery of their daily promenade. They would have liked to walk to the mall by themselves, as they were accustomed to doing, back in Nanjing. But the streets there are much wider, and safer. There were much bigger sidewalks, flanked by the rich foliage of mature trees.

Here, the roads are hilly, with no pedestrian walks. Cars race by at 40-plus miles an hour. In addition, they didn't speak much English (Han Mama's English would not be enough for them to survive any real-life emergency situations), and we were worried about their safety even though we live in a relatively safe, middle-class suburb. With their "safety and health" high in our minds, we had to veto their idea for territorial expansion.

Han Mama, a former Distinguished Teacher with "peaches and plums all over the world," soon reconnected with many of her former students working, studying and living in the United States. They would call in from all points between New York and Los Angeles. Once she mastered the how-to of making long distance calls in America, she would pick up the phone, dial the number and call them in return.

She would call a distant cousin of hers in Flushing, New York, a daughter of her late husband's sister in Paris and the sister back in China. Oh, she could really chat. She would chat on and on, often in a dialect that sounded much like a bird's language. And there I was, sitting upstairs in the little office, trying to concentrate with this bird twittering below.

The in-laws were somewhat different from my parents. In fact, they were different from most Chinese parents. They were full of new ideas. They were even entrepreneurial. They had planned to make somewhere between 3000 or 4000 dollars by having Han Mama teach or tutor kids in Chinese. She did teach a couple of classes at the weekend Chinese school my wife ran. But that school was just beginning, was volunteer-based, and there was no pay.

She soon complained of insomnia as a result of strenuous mental efforts in preparing lessons, and we had to abandon the idea of having a real professional teaching the kids Chinese for the summer. But she passionately believed in Chinese kids keeping up their own cultural heritage. So she continued to teach Chinese to our son at home, and his Chinese, by the time they were leaving, sounded much more like authentic Chinese. He could even write in Chinese. We were very happy.

Once they felt safe and healthy, and sightseeing became something of a routine, the in-laws began to look across the Atlantic, and feel the allure of Paris. That daughter of her late husband's sister was doing great in Paris, her husband being a prominent businessman in the Chinese community there. Besides, before leaving for America, Han Mama had been told by a fortune-teller that she was destined to make a tour of the world. I wasn't thrilled, however, by the prospect of them vacationing in Paris. I was worried about Father-in-law's high blood pressure and heart conditions. I was worried about Han Mama not knowing how to say one single word in French. Besides, nobody there had issued an all-expenses-paid invitation to them as we had done for their visit to America.

But I complied and began to explore the possibility for them to travel to Paris. I surfed on the Internet and checked the websites for the State Department, the Office of Immigration and Naturalization, and the French Embassy. I found out that it would be rather difficult for a citizen of the People's Republic of China to get a visa, and that once they were in Paris—if they could get the visa at all—they would not be able to re-enter the United States. It would mean that they would have to take all their luggage with them to Paris, and would have to buy another two plane tickets to fly back to Shanghai, thus wasting half of the round trip tickets we had already bought them.

Facing these insurmountable obstacles, they reluctantly turned their gaze back to this side of the Atlantic.

The In-Laws are Coming!

Then, one of Han Mama's former students from Long Island invited them over. They had just had a baby. His wife was depressed because she had to stay home all day, she had no support from her family network, and she was inexperienced in child rearing. The in-laws decided to go and help them. This time, there was nothing to stop them.

Once they got there, Han Mama appropriated the kitchen as her own domain: she cleaned up their fridge and cabinets, and cooked a delicious dinner with all the proper nutritional and medicinal values. She also shared all her child rearing secrets with the new mother.

Father-in-law was also very happy for the change of locale. Here, he could wander around almost as freely as he used to back in Nanjing. When I eventually went to pick them up, they were reluctant to leave. Han Mama's student and his wife almost begged for them to stay longer.

During their stay in Long Island, they also had a chance to visit Han Mama's distant cousin in Flushing. The cousin had come to the U. S. several years before, was on welfare and living in a government subsidized one-bedroom apartment in a housing project. The 10th floor apartment was tidy, had heat and all the basic appliances, and commanded a very good view of the surrounding area. There was also a clean and well-maintained little park not far from her building. There, residents could sit, relax, and chat with each other.

The in-laws were so impressed with it all even though they have a rather roomy, well-furnished, 3-bedroom apartment back in Nanjing. They would never have believed it if they had not seen it with their own eyes that the poor and downtrodden could enjoy such "luxuries" almost free in the United States, a "man-eating-man" capitalist society! This is much more socialist than a socialist country such as China. Of course, I didn't dare take them to places where stark poverty has driven people to utter despair.

There was one little unexpected interlude during their stay in Long Island: the U.S. fired missiles on the suspected bases of Osama Bin Ladin in Afghanistan. The morning after, Father-in-law saw a big headline in a local Chinese newspaper: Terrorists Threaten Retaliation in New York. As a WWII veteran with several bullet holes in his body, he was concerned.

He had seen the TV footage of the carnage inflicted upon the two U.S. embassies in Africa. His blood pressure shot way up. He wanted us to get his luggage to Long Island so that they could go to JFK, board a plane and return to China. After all, he hadn't included this terrorist attack in the itinerary for his trip to America.

Over the phone, I tried to calm him down. Nothing much would happen, I said, particularly at this time when the crisis was still unfolding, and with security already having been beefed up. If anything was going to happen, I continued, it would be a year or two later, when the vigilance was low, because they like to strike—bang!—when and where you were least expecting them to.

He felt somewhat better. His blood pressure fell back close to its normal level. But he instructed that I should avoid driving through the downtown areas in New York on my way to get them back to our safe home in Pennsylvania.

Not long after their return, however, they began to think of Long Island again. Oh, Han Mama missed so much the fresh crab they had caught there, and Father-in-law missed the beaches where he would stroll freely. Besides, they could help the young couple with the small baby. Then, they could go directly to JFK when it was time, and board the plane home.

We would not say yes. We were busy and didn't have time to drive them—about four to five hours each way—back and forth between Long Island, NY and Harrisburg, PA again. My fall semester had already begun. My wife had a full-time job, was running a weekend Chinese language school and was preparing for a big medical technologist license test. Besides, we didn't deem it proper for them to leave America without us—their children—seeing them off at JFK. So they spent their last week more or less confined in our home: there was not much in the way of sightseeing or weekend short trips anywhere. They were being neglected.

Then, the packing for their return trip began. There were four bags altogether, full of things they had bought for themselves, Han Mama's kids, their close friends and the things we had bought for them. Han Mama was in charge of it all. Somehow, she was not eager to squeeze in the few small gifts my wife had prepared for one of our nieces—her brother's daughter (her parents had divorced), or the few small bottles of Alaskan deep sea fish oil—a recent fad in China—we had bought for my mother. The bags were too full already and would be too heavy for Father-in-law to manage, she explained apologetically.

The In-Laws are Coming! 89

Father-in-law intervened. He would not break his back at Shanghai International Airport, he reassured, because her daughter and son-in-law would be waiting at the foot of the gangway ladder dutifully. She acquiesced reluctantly.

The night before their departure, Father-in-law made a farewell speech over a table full of delicious dishes, giving a thumbs-up for their visit to America. Then Han Mama addressed the table. After echoing Father-in-law's positive evaluation, she said—rather to my surprise—what she had worried the most before the trip was me, her new stepson-in-law. She had been anxious whether I would accept her. Now she realized all that worry and anxiety had not been necessary because during the four-month stay she felt as comfortable with me as with her own son.

When the speech making was over, Father-in-law took out six very new hundred dollar bills from his pocket and wanted us to accept them: "This is from Han Mama and me. It's a little token of our heartfelt appreciation." We rejected profusely and the bills traveled back and forth between us many times. But they would not take the money back.

I was gripped with a sense of guilt. I regretted that I had not said yes when they wanted to go to Paris, or when they wanted to revisit Long Island. I wished that I had said yes when they hinted that they'd like to come and attend our son's high school graduation in a few years.

Isn't it the duty of any good Chinese to make their parents happy, even if their happiness would require making a tour of the world? Have I lived in America too long to remember my filial duty as a son-in-law? Have I become petty and parsimonious?

One o'clock in the afternoon the next day at JFK, we had checked in their luggage. We had said goodbye to each other one last time. Father-in-law and Han Mama began to walk through the security checkpoint. Then, they walked slowly toward Gate 5 where they would board their plane, Han Mama's right arm around Father-in-law's waist. She seemed less buoyant and somewhat smaller than before, and her back bent a bit more. They turned and waved to us a few times.

My wife and I stood on this side of the security, speechless, and watched them gradually become a blurry outline, and finally disappear into Gate 5. I felt a little lump in my throat as my eyes began to leak.

Part II
The Tango

Sino-American Tango

Taiwan Strait Crisis: More Complex Than Morality Play

MARCH 17, 1996

THIS IS NOT THE BRIGHTEST OF TIMES. This is not the darkest of times. But the heart of anyone altruistically or practically concerned about the Taiwan Strait would be chilled by the smoke from the live missile exercises there, and the shadows of aircraft carriers looming nearby. Another major confrontation seems imminent.

Much of the media in this country has portrayed this crisis as another episode of a "Good guys versus Bad guys" morality play on the world's political stage. However, with a vantage point gained not only through the satellite access to media from mainland China, Taiwan and Hong Kong, but also through having lived long enough on both sides of the Pacific, I fail to see it as so obvious and crystal-clear.

It's true that Taiwan is on its epoch-making march towards democracy, which will soon culminate in its first popularly-elected president. It's also true that much of this process has been severely contaminated, as known to all Taiwan people, by the permeation of the "dark" (the gangland) and the "gold" (the money).

It may be true that the current Taiwan president, Mr. Li Denghui, is a patriotic hero, as is presented by the media here, because of his instrumental role in Taiwan's efforts to shake off its long, totalitarian chain. It's also true, as has been well documented by his opponents in Taiwan, that this image is tarnished by his political trickery and distrustful nature, and his publicly professed nostalgia for the days when Taiwan was colonized by imperialist Japan before the end of WWII.

It's true that Mr. Li has repeatedly promised to uphold the "One China" policy, and that it is reckless for the mainland to play war games right at the front door of the island. It's also true that this latest episode is not caused, as alleged, by the democratic election there, but directly by Li's "alumnae diplomacy," "visa diplomacy," "vacation diplomacy," "stop-over diplomacy," and what have you, the undisguised agenda of which is to ultimately sever the island from the mainland.

It's true that the apparently unbridgeable differences between the political systems, the long history of hostility and distrust, and the prosperity on the one side and the Third World status on the other, make a reunification seem implausible. It's also true that people on both sides are descendants of the Dragon, sharing the same umbilical cord anthropologically, culturally, and linguistically, and that the majority of them do not want to see these blood ties summarily broken—just talk to my friends from both Taiwan and the mainland here. It's also true that with the economic boom on the mainland, and the slow but sure arrival of democracy there, reunification has become both desirable and inevitable—sooner or later.

Will the arrival of the carriers *Independence* and *Nimitz* help ease the mounting tension there? It may and it may not. A single spark or act of aggression could well start a hellish fire from which no one will escape unscorched. There would be no glorious withdrawal. Besides, to the 1.2 billion nervous systems intensely charged by the memory in their collective conscious and unconscious of the humiliations forced upon them by outside powers, the arrival of these carriers must only serve to remind them of the countless foreign warships and gunboats that have sheared through their harbors and rivers since the Opium Wars.

To the Chinese, the siren-song of the so-called "China Threat" is nothing but a bastard variant of the centuries old "yellow peril" corpse, resurrected to meet the insatiable psychological need for melodrama, and practical need for a new villain to fill the void left by the bygone "Evil Empire." The fact is that with the exceptions of a few border dispute clashes, China's modern history since 1840 is not one of aggression, but one of notorious violation.

This comment is not meant to advocate for the "devil," or for absolute moral relativism and anarchy, but to point out the fact that the current crisis in the Taiwan Strait is much more complex than the simple, good vs. bad morality play.

Being politically naive, I'd like to see a quick and smooth end to this strange and surreal interlude: no more taunting from one side of the Taiwan Strait, and no more bullying from the other side. I'd like to see the beginning of respectful and constructive dialogue toward peaceful coexistence and towards eventual peaceful reunification. As we approach the dawn of the next millennium, if we are too stupid to be able to create the brightest of times in our time, at least we can and should use whatever wisdom left us to avoid ushering in the darkest of the times.

Mutual Engagement Best for U.S. and China

April 17, 1996

THE WAR GAMES ARE OVER, the ballots have been counted, and a president has been elected peacefully. The aircraft carriers are turning around, sailing to other waters. The specter of a bloody conflict, having hovered over the Taiwan Strait for a while, has all but evaporated.

Before the skies have completely cleared up, conciliatory overtures have already been made from both sides of the Strait. Suddenly, there is a renewal of hope.

We can all sigh with relief. For now.

However, a renewal of long-stagnant, Sino-American relations is still slow in coming. Indeed, to hear the recent "big stick" rhetoric of Cold War warriors, one would assume that it would serve the best interests of the world to begin the Cold War all over again. Such rhetoric can only be conjured up out of a misunderstanding of the complex nature of the long history of Sino-American relations.

From the time America and China came into direct contact, right after the English gunboats blasted open the door of the proud but xenophobic Asian giant, their relationships have often been entangled in what I would characterize, for lack of a better metaphor, as a "multi-partner tango."

Tugged by strings of discordant geopolitical and ideological priorities, commercial interests, modes of government, domestic partisan politics and historical and cultural heritages, this "tango" has been anything but graceful, with a lot of stepping on each other's toes. In all these years, China, because of her backwardness, has often been treated as a big, but contemptible junior partner.

The clumsiness of the partners aside, this "tango" can be dangerous and even catastrophic when it turns into an ego contest. A case in point would be the Korean War. Painful as the subject is, it would do no harm to remind ourselves of a lesson we can learn today. As documented by prominent historians in this country, even after Kim Il-Sung's military adventure, and the brilliantly executed Inchon landing, and notwithstanding the geopolitical and ideological antagonisms, China and U. S. might not have met in the battlefield had Premier Zhou's warning about U.S. not to cross the 38th parallel been received and weighed properly, had Truman not given a free hand to the popular two-world-war hero, General MacArthur, to march across the line towards China-Korea border, and had Mao with his equally larger-than-life personality not dominated other Politburo members who were initially doubtful of sending "volunteers" across the Yalu River.

It can be speculated that with a direct and more effective high-level dialogue, the thousands of American and millions of Korean and Chinese lives might not have been wasted in a war from the ruins of which no clear winner emerged.

To avoid letting history repeat itself, U. S. and China should continue to seek "mutual comprehension" and "constructive engagement" with each other instead of playing more Cold War games.

The first time I flew the friendly skies of America, it was on a cold, snowy January night from San Francisco to Chicago. The view outside the window was a dark, mysterious unknown: alluring and threatening at the same time. The second time I flew, however, it was on a warm, sunny, crystal clear afternoon in mid May that same year, from Chicago to Boston. I was enchanted by the breath-taking view below: it was indeed "America the Beautiful."

Of course, true understanding and appreciation does not come from traversing the skies over a country a couple of times. Equally, policies that have enormous bilateral and global repercussions should not be based upon half-digested knowledge gleaned from a carry out box of egg rolls, wonton soup, princess chicken, and yes, the indispensable fortune cookies, or fleeting footage on CBS, or ABC. Neither should eating hot dogs, apple pies, playing golf, driving Chevrolets and watching translated "True Lies" be counted as real understanding of another culture.

Mutual Engagement Best for U.S. and China

Realistically, many of the geopolitical and ideological barriers can not be surmounted in the foreseeable future. Nevertheless, there are many areas where the two countries could cooperate extensively for their mutual benefit, especially at a time when both are up to their ears in challenges. China is being hampered by outdated and overworked infrastructures, rampant corruption, the widening gap between the upstart rich and the hard-working poor, and between the booming coastal regions and the grumbling central and western provinces being left behind. This is not even to mention the challenge of feeding and clothing a population *five times* that of the U.S. with about *one-fifth* of its arable land. Even though the population has not grown geometrically as a gloomy Malthus predicted, and China has met the challenge with success so far, subsistence often hangs by a thread. This delicate eco-system is too easily ravaged by major natural disasters.

America's challenges have been paraded dazzlingly in the by now almost forgotten "Contract with America" signed unilaterally by yesteryear's victorious Republicans. On top of that should be added the "enough-is-*not*-enough" downsizing of profitable, corporate Goliaths and the ever-present threat of nuclear proliferation in many parts of the world.

Neither side can afford to enter another Cold War. If friendship between China and the U.S. is to be a "what-you-want-is-what-you-get" situation, and not an uncertain box of chocolates, the choice should be obvious to both. It should also be obvious that there will be no stability and prosperity without constructive engagement. There will be no constructive engagement without mutual comprehension, and there would be no mutual comprehension without an appreciation of the complex bilateral and global interdependence the two countries are enmeshed in.

China has finally grown into an almost equal partnership in this "multi-partner tango," and should be treated accordingly to avoid stepping on each other's toes and heading into a catastrophic collision. The stick-and-carrot diplomacy, which has an odor of the bygone era, and an air of condescension to a lesser partner, has become a near anachronism.

While "big stick" rhetoric may provide an adrenaline rush, especially in an election year, we all know that one Cold War all but consumed us.

Did You Hear a Clash?

JANUARY 1, 1997

SOMETHING THERE IS that doesn't love the word "clash." This I found out recently when I joined the Elmo-maniac crowds in a local mall and drifted into a chain book store to buy a new book that had been hailed by pundits like Henry Kissinger as "one of the most important books to have emerged since the end of the Cold War."

I searched for it among the Hot Books, Cool Gifts, Best-sellers, and the newest Crichtons and Clancys, to no avail. I was in an excited state of mind, and my patience was a bit short in supply. So I cut my fruitless searching short, and approached a young salesclerk for assistance.

"Sure, I'll look it up in the computer," he responded enthusiastically. "Samuel P. Huntington, " he vocalized the reference I was giving him while delivering staccato strokes on the keyboard, "*The Clash of Civilizations and the Remaking of World Order.* Yes, we've got it!"

He marched to a loaded shelf among loaded shelves and, from its lowest rung, dug out a book wrapped in a dark, ominous-looking jacket. "That's it," I confirmed.

While swiping my credit card through the cash register, he remarked, conversationally, "you know what, you're the first person to buy this book, and it's our only copy."

Ah! What a letdown after all this frenzy!

The main thesis of Huntington's highly acclaimed new book goes like this: with the beginning of the post-Cold War era, global politics is in the process of being reconfigured along civilizational (religious, cultural, and ethnic) instead of ideological lines. As a result, the fault lines between major civilizations (the "arrogant" West, the "intolerant" Islamic, the "assertive" Confucian, etc.) are becoming the central lines of conflict, and will probably, if not inevitably, lead to major inter-civilizational wars in the early 21st century, particularly between the challenger Confucian, and the dominant but fading Western civilizations.

Did You Hear a Clash? 99

Of course, Huntington, a prominent Harvard professor, director of the John M. Olin Institute for Strategic Studies and chairman of the Harvard Academy for International and Area Studies, is by no means one of those *fin de siécle* augurs, or doomsday soothsayers. Much less is he a tormented hate-mongering and jingoistic maniac. His 367, densely-illustrated pages, with another 40 pages of meticulously documented endnotes, are ample testimony to his scholastic prowess and moral seriousness.

Yet, something there is that doesn't love the word "clash."

Whenever I turn the pages of human history and the annals of this 20th century, my heart is overfilled with joy, pride, and gratefulness for all the miraculous discoveries, marvelous inventions and magnificent achievements: the *raison d'tre* for *homo sapiens* on this Earth.

Sad that the same act of review can make me burn with shame, too. Those same pages are indelibly stained by bloody wars, urged on by sheer greed, hatred, ignorance, misunderstanding and often times misguided, fanatical self-righteousness. Precious few have been fought for what could be termed "just causes." In the 20th century alone, the figures for war-related human sacrifices have reached astronomical scales, which is common knowledge to even elementary school kids.

Evidently, the "civilizing" process hasn't done much to tame the wild, "barbaric" instincts in our nature.

Of course, Huntington may have his finger on something here. Among scholars of different persuasions, there is a grudging consensus that the axis of the globe is gradually tilting toward the East in what John Naisbitt has termed a "megashift" of economic and political power. With the renewed power comes a growing sense of "Asianness," among the heterogeneous nation-states across that part of the world. Meanwhile, there has been a discernible "resurgence" among Islamic countries to turn to Islam "as a source of identity, meaning, stability, legitimacy, development, power, and hope."

It is also true that language, religion, and racial and ethnic origins are among the deepest values whereby individuals, groups, communities, and even nations identify themselves. But people of different civilizations, and civilizations themselves for that matter, have to learn how to live with each other, and how to live and let live. This proves to be particularly hard for one who has been used to the role of a big brother and who now feels challenged.

Besides cleaning up its own house of "moral decay" and "cultural suicide," one major strategy Huntington has proposed for the West to retain its dominance is the old "divide and conquer" policy, playing off nation-states of other civilizations against one another. This seems to be a recipe for another Cold War. Pursued aggressively, it could lead to exactly that which it purports to avert.

Given the world as it is today, with the proliferation of nukes, a major inter-civilizational war would not be the war to end all wars, but a war to end all civilizations.

We've got to find more "civilized" ways than wars to deal with inter-civilizational differences as well as ideological quarrels and distribution of limited resources. We can and are obligated to ourselves to prove that even pundits can sometimes be wrong.

Yes, something there is that doesn't love the word "clash." Maybe, it's the happy, jolly holiday spirit. Maybe, the sound of the word itself is too harsh and jarring for the ear. The word "peace" rings much more pleasant, and may it ring in the new millennium!

Whatever it is, that book store might just as well leave its inventory incomplete. The swan song chanted by that renowned scholar for the West, and indeed for all civilizations, has already depressed one reader badly enough. And a thousand apologies for passing on some of that depressing note with you at this happy jolly time of the year, but I thought you should hear what some renowned scholars are saying about your world.

You know what, I've earned myself a break, and am going to do something much lighter for this holiday season: I want to tickle the famed Elmo's tummy.

Just once, mind you...

A Bridge into the 21st Century

NOVEMBER 5, 1997

IT WAS FEBRUARY 21ST, 1972 at the Beijing Airport. Before emerging from the door of Air Force One and walking down the ramp, Richard M. Nixon had ordered his aides to block the aisle of the plane to prevent other officials from following too closely. As the first American president to ever visit the world's most populous country—not only since it was "lost" to the Communists in 1949—Nixon wanted to make sure that the triumph of such a historical moment was not shared with anyone else.

When Jiang Zemin, President of the People's Republic, emerged from his special plane in Honolulu on Oct. 26, 1997, he probably didn't need to issue such orders to his aides. Being good Chinese, they knew exactly where their place was at such a moment in history. Moreover, however important it was, Jiang's visit was not a historical breakthrough in any sense of the term as Nixon's had been 25 years ago.

Before Nixon walked down the ramp, the two countries had been estranged from each other for over two decades. For the United States, the visit would tip the global balance of power much in its favor: it would enable the U.S. to pull out of an ugly and unwinable war in Vietnam with as much dignity as was left. It would further strengthen its position in pursuing *détente* with the Soviet Union by holding the "China Card."

For China, inviting Nixon to visit would mean reconnecting with the outside world after decades of isolation, both self-imposed and externally forced upon, and it would mean being able to play the American Card in counterbalancing the military threat along its hundreds of miles of border with the Soviet Union.

Today, however, neither the United States nor China is facing any serious domestic or international crisis of comparable magnitude by anyone's estimation. The Cold War is over and no mutual enemy is anywhere in sight.

Nevertheless, the significance of Jiang's visit should not be underestimated either.

Since Nixon's visit and the eventual normalization in 1979 during Carter's presidency, U.S.-China relations have experienced periodic progress and stagnation, falling to a low point after the tragedy at Tiananmen Square in 1989. The most explosive moment, largely unnoticed by average Americans busy with their everyday routine, was during last year's Taiwan Strait crisis when China and the U.S. were on the verge of a major military showdown.

Such an erratic and unpredictable pattern of relationship between the only superpower in the world today, and the other up-and-coming superpower is not only dangerous for the two countries themselves, but also dangerous for all the countries in the Asian Pacific region and the whole world.

Thus, Jiang's visit signifies that the leaders of both countries have finally come to appreciate the vital importance of a stable, mature and constructive relationship not only between the U.S. and China, but also towards the world at large as it marches into the 21st century. The two countries may not have been, and may never develop into best friends, but guided by such a historical and strategic vision, they can cooperate responsibly and productively in many important areas and deal with serious differences, ideological and economic, without risking direct confrontation.

To many, Jiang's visit is only symbolic, but in this case the symbolism is substantial.

Still, the success of such a long-term strategic partnership is contingent upon clear, mutual understanding.

When the fanfare—the 21-cannon salute, red carpet, toasting, etc.—is over, Jiang should realize how dearly Americans cherish freedom and democracy. He should understand that these ideals go deeper than simply being able to recite "Fourscore and seven years ago," donning a colonial hat, or touring Independence Hall.

Jiang argues that a comprehensive definition of human rights should mean, first and foremost, the rights to social and economic development. This is a valid argument for the simple reason that China is inhabited by one fifth of the world's population, and this huge chunk of humanity needs adequate food, shelter, and access to education, employment and health care. Yet that argument can be carried only to a point.

The speed of economic development and its achievement has pushed China well beyond the threshold of subsistence. Time is ripe for China to embark on serious political reforms. The Chinese government should understand that such

A Bridge into the 21st Century

reforms, if carried out gradually, would not hinder economic development or disrupt unity and stability, which happen to be highly cherished Chinese values. Instead, people would be happier if they were free to exercise their civil and political rights. In addition, political reform would enhance the opportunity for a peaceful solution to the Taiwan issue.

When Jiang is back in China, it would do him no harm if he loses sleep over the "noisy" drum beating and slogan shouting he encountered during the visit.

Americans, for their part, have a lot to learn about China, too. To the overwhelming majority of the Chinese, this may be the best of times in the last few centuries. Right now, they—understandably—care more about improving their living conditions than gaining the right to protest or print unflattering cartoons of the president of their country. Besides, because of the humiliations China suffered at the hands of foreign powers in modern times, both the people and the government do not like to bow down to any outside pressure.

While many of the problems facing China today have complex social, economic and historical underpinnings, some are not too difficult to understand. Take family planning, for example. All one needs to do is to close his or her eyes, and imagine the population in the United States suddenly increased five times over, and then imagine the ensuing consequences.

As to the problem of Tibet, it is much more complex than what is portrayed in a couple of movies made by Hollywood. While Hollywood has no rival in being the best entertainer, its self-acquired role of moral leadership, and arbiter of international affairs, should at least be taken with a grain of salt.

To really understand China means going on trips, as the one to be led by a colleague of mine next summer, to see China with an open mind, and with one's own eyes.

If President Clinton has been musing a great deal lately as to what his administration's legacy will be, he has good reasons to rest assured now. The precedent set by Richard Nixon, who despite Watergate and so many self-incriminating tapes being released, is still remembered as the president who "regained" China, finds affinities with the Clinton years. After all the flip-flops in his China policies, Clinton has finally had a vision, and has decided to lead instead of simply following the polls.

The result of such a vision is a new strategic partnership between the U.S. and China, or a bridge, to use a favorite metaphor of Clinton's, into the 21st century.

Leadership

JULY 5, 1998

I AM NOT A FAN. It's hard to be his fan anyway, with all the shameless, blush-inducing graphic details of all the scandals, alleged or real, constantly bombarding your eardrums and eyeballs.

He has been accused of being a "spineless chaser of polls," rather than a leader with vision, but President Clinton did show leadership this time by deciding to embark on an historical trip to China. Had he listened to the cacophony drummed up by partisan politics naysayers, sheer ignorance, greed for ratings, votes and drama as well as some legitimate concerns that dominated the nation's airwaves, he would have stayed in the Oval Office. From there, he would have watched his name and image juxtaposed with that of a star-struck, ex-intern (and her disloyal friend-confidant) on the front page every day. He would also have been haunted by subpoenas, served up by a high-minded, but equally Starrdom-seeking special prosecutor. It would have been a summer of discontent.

Instead, he went to China, accompanied by his loving wife and dutiful daughter, and an entourage of over 1000 officials, business people and journalists. There, he immersed himself in the warm embrace of one of the oldest and richest civilizations in the world. There he was given an imperial welcome in the ancient city of Xian in Central China, wandering, awe-struck, among the rank and file of the 2,200-year-old, fully armored, terra cotta warriors.

In Beijing, he strolled freely on the ten-thousand *li* Great Wall, famed as the only man-made object visible from the outer space. In Shanghai, he caught a brief glimpse of Pudong, poised to be the Manhattan of China, only newer and cleaner.

But the Clintons were not there on holiday, visiting for the purpose of escaping and recuperating from the traumatizing domestic politics, or to fulfill one of his long-cherished childhood wishes. They were in China as representatives of the presidency of the United States of America. His detractors had already written off his trip, even before Air Force One took off from Dulles, calling it everything from a cowardly attempt to divert attention from his personal crisis, to empty symbolism,

Leadership 105

to "Operation Humiliation" (as coined by a notorious radio talk show host). Regardless of the initial perception, the president had indeed gone to China with a mission—and a message. The mission was to nurture a mature and constructive relationship between the biggest developed nation, and the biggest developing nation. Like it or not, much of the world's peace, stability and prosperity in the first century of the next millennium may depend on how the two big powers behave towards each other.

This was the message President Clinton delivered by taking the trip, conducting the joint press conference with President Jiang of China, and in giving a speech to the best and brightest at the Peking University. During the press conference, he debated in unequivocal, yet polite language, with President Jiang on such sensitive issues as human rights, Tiananmen Square and Tibet.

At Peking University, he explained in an engaging and professorial style why political liberties would eventually help China achieve its goal of becoming an even greater country. The students were certainly impressed though they may not have been completely convinced, as indicated by the pointed questions they put to the American president. Questions such as: Isn't it double standard for the United States to condemn China of weapons trade while it itself has been the most aggressive and biggest exporter of weapons of mass destruction?

Both the press conference and the speech were broadcast live—a historical first for China. Judging from the number of TV sets in China, as many as 800 million eagerly watched. Though the exchange of views may not have been spirited enough to satisfy the taste buds of folks here in the U.S., who are quite desensitized to political drama, it must have been extremely exciting to the Chinese viewers, who have come to accept censored media as a fact of life. The repercussions of this live broadcast are likely more far-reaching than anyone has yet contemplated. Time will tell.

Despite all the differences, Clinton sees the potential for constructive cooperation between the two countries: a vision that serves their respective best interests. While a candidate in 1992, Clinton lacked such vision, much as candidate Reagan lacked in the late 70s, but sought to correct later, during his presidency. Now, in seeing the strategic importance of the relationship, Clinton's vision is shared by almost all the living and able-minded former presidents, Secretaries of State and Defense and National Security Advisors. You would almost have to be an incurable conspiracy theory junkie to see this as "another sellout" by an elected, or appointed, servant of the United States.

In order to understand why China is what it is today politically, socially, economically and culturally, one must delve into the history of China since the 1840 Opium War, as a group of Penn State University students have recently done in a modern Chinese history class I taught. Anyone who has visited China recently, as the group of professors and students who have just returned from a trip organized by a colleague of mine, would be able to appreciate the tremendous changes that have occurred and are occurring in China in almost all facets of life.

China is in a crucial transitional stage in its history. It has yet to significantly broaden its citizens' political liberties, and it is facing enormous social, economic and environmental challenges. As many of my Chinese friends here, and no doubt millions of Chinese at home agree, while China needs a more democratic system in order to realize its ambitious goals of reclaiming its "past glory" (a Clintonism from his recent visit), any shock approach to political reform would more than likely lead to chaos. In addition, China has to find a democratic system that works best for its people.

As President Clinton acknowledges, there are more millennia in Chinese history than there are centuries in U.S. history. If you consider yourself fair and open-minded, if you have some sense of history and if you are endowed with the virtue of patience, you will be able to appreciate the fact that China is much freer than it ever had been, and is opening up its borders faster than many in the U.S. realize. This would not have happened if a policy of isolation and containment—similar to those pursued in the 50s and 60s—had been continued.

Many in the U.S. have been crying for leadership, and have been complaining that President Clinton runs the country according to poll results. Now that he has decided to lead with vision, these same folks are crying foul again. They seem to have their minds made up about Clinton, and would not be happy no matter what he did. But I have lived long enough in this country to recognize true leadership when it is shown. I think I'm ready to join his fan club, at least for the time being.

Frenzied Fallacies

APRIL 11, 1999

FALLACIES ARE STATEMENTS, or arguments that have gone awry because they are based on false or invalid inferences.

Recent hoopla over China, Chinese-Americans, and the alleged nuclear espionage, has been cooked up by the mainstream media on the prowl for sensational stories in order to relieve the post-Monica (and pre-Kosovo) boredom, can be characterized just as such.

FALLACY #1: China has stolen sensitive nuclear weapon technology. Despite the hysteria over the alleged sensitive high-tech theft, all that is known is that in the 1980s, Dr. Lee, a Taiwan-born American scientist, with the prior approval of proper authorities at the Los Alamos Lab in New Mexico, went to Hong Kong and Beijing to attend a few conferences with his fellow nuclear scientists. Did he leak any bomb-making secrets, deliberately or inadvertently? It has never been established. Nor is there the slightest evidence that he was recruited by China. Indeed, according to law enforcement officials, investigations at other nuclear labs so far have either "collapsed" or "found no evidence of espionage." They have expressed "sharp skepticism" about the seriousness of other emerging cases.

Nevertheless, sucked into the frenzy it has created, the media, along with the Cold-Warriors in Congress, are still tearing their hair out, and expending much hot air over this as if it were a proven fact. And Dr. Lee, of course, has already been crucified, without due process.

FALLACY #2: There is a vast Chinese-American espionage network in the U. S. It's more than disconcerting to hear such paranoiac nonsense from the talking heads of the mainstream media. Chinese Americans, whether born in mainland China, Taiwan, or here, are hardworking, family-loving and law-abiding members of society. They not only cherish their ties with the land of their origin and their rich cultural heritages, but also love their new homes here. The last thing they want to see is a strained relationship—heaven forbid a war—between China and the U.S. Many have worked hard to help bridge the differences and promote understanding between people of the two countries. The broad-brush painting of them as (potential) spies casts a long and depressing shadow over their lives and careers here, and is totally uncalled for, groundless, and irresponsible. Again, they are being condemned for no less than their ethnicity.

The paranoia reveals a deep-rooted distrust on the part of the mainstream society towards immigrants coming from other shores of the Pacific. When it is politically expedient, it would showcase Chinese and Asian-American success stories, parading these people as model minorities. Of course, it is often done to silence other minorities who are struggling for equality and a level playing field. The next moment, this country can turn around, and accuse the same people of questionable loyalty. Who knows what could happen to them if one day a war (God forbid!) broke out between the two countries? Will the interment camps of the 1940s re-open?

These fallacies are derivatives of a number of other fallacies, among which are the following two.

FALLACY #3: China is a rogue state, undertaking a huge military buildup for its hegemonic ambitions. Even authors of *Coming Conflict with China* (1997)—choirboys of the "China Threat" chorus—admit that China, unlike the former Soviet Union, is not a "territorially and ideologically expansionist country with a rigidly controlled economy and a messianic, world-conquering vision of itself." At least, it "has no intention of sending its troops to conquer the territory of other Asian countries."

Records show that China has acted responsibly since it rejoined the world community early in the 1970s. It has played an essential role in bringing a peaceful resolution to the mess in Cambodia, has been constructive in containing the potentially explosive situation on the Korean peninsula, and instrumental in defusing the recent nuclear crisis between India and Pakistan. It also acted responsibly during the Asian financial crisis by resisting the temptation to devalue its currency. While a devaluation would have helped China regain its competitiveness in exports, it would certainly have thrown the jittery Asian economy into another tailspin.

It is true that China has accelerated its efforts to modernize its military, but as security analysts in this country have pointed out, China has been thus engaged out of rather grim geo-strategic necessities. It has one of the worst security environments in the world, sharing thousands of miles of borders

Frenzied Fallacies

with 14 other nations. Through peaceful negotiations, significant progress has been made in solving border disputes between China and its neighbors. Most of these disputes are left over from complicated historical circumstances.

Moreover, China's military expenditure pales in comparison to its vast size, and to similar expenditures of other countries. In Fiscal Year 1996, for example, even by the most inflated estimate, China's defense budget was $44.4 billion. This figure is much less than that of Japan, a much smaller island country which by its "peace constitution" is supposed to maintain only a small military force for self-defense.

Since early 1990s, the annual bill for the much-hyped Chinese purchase of advanced technology from Russia has been about $1 to 2 billion. How does this figure compare to the $11.99 billion the U.S. military paid to one of its defense contractors, Lockheed Martin, in Fiscal Year 1996, alone?

When you look at the plain facts, all the hysteria coming over the airwaves about China dropping nukes on American cities, when it is the only member of the nuclear club that has officially pledged never to be the first to strike, becomes perplexing.

FALLACY #4: China is a Totalitarian Communist State. "Totalitarian" and "communist" are among the scariest labels that one can throw at you in this country because of the nightmarish pictures of red or white terror they conjure up. Applying such labels to today's China, however, is not only inaccurate, but also intellectually lazy and disingenuous.

Any responsible watcher of recent developments in China can tell you that China has become much less ideological and much more interested in social and economic development. The word "Communism" has been virtually out of circulation over there for quite some time now. In fact, China has been engaged in perhaps one of the largest experiments in grossroots democracy in history, searching for that better form of government that would best fit.

Granted that China is not—and may never develop into—a democracy in the American sense of the term. Furthermore, it needs to push more aggressively for political reforms, even though it has already made significant progress in improving both the social and economic life of its people. Only a few weeks ago, while the paranoiac hoopla was raging on right here, China's People's Congress took up the monumental task of revising its constitution, formally adopting market economy, rule of law, and private enterprises into its social, economic, and political system.

Even with the state-controlled media, I have noticed a considerable level of freedom and aggressiveness with which journalists question government officials over policy issues. It's not quite the kind of "grilling" their American counterparts employ, but give it time.

All these developments, expectedly, are not newsworthy to the mainstream media here, but they continue to set precedents that are quickly adopted by others.

To some folks, the problem they have with China is not Communism, totalitarianism or its human rights record, but the fact that it has a different culture. Samuel Huntington makes this very clear in his book *Clash of Civilizations* (1996).

The word "fallacy" in its Latin origin means "deceive." A deceitful statement or argument can be made either intentionally, or out of carelessness and sheer ignorance. The mainstream media would certainly bristle at the charge of carelessness and ignorance. As to their Cold-War buddies in Congress, whether they have intentionally drummed up the hysteria 1) to get even with Clinton over the defeat of their impeachment attempt, 2) to scare the American people into supporting a resurrection of the dead-on-arrival Star Wars program, or, 3) to galvanize their campaign to take back the White House in the year 2000, I leave to the readers' own judgement.

One thing is clear, though: U.S.-China relations are rather fragile, and if one side pushes too hard, a potential friendship can quickly turn into enmity.

The irresponsible yellow journalism and Cold War-mongering have got to stop.

Fraility, Thy Name is—

MAY 19, 1999

AS A CHINESE LIVING in the United States, I have a vested interest in following the reactions—both in China and in the United States—to the recent American bombing of the Chinese embassy in Yugoslavia. What I have seen, I tell you, is quite surreal and oftentimes frustrating. I have gained a keener appreciation of how frail the U.S.-China relationship can be, and how difficult it is for the Chinese and the Americans to really understand each other.

First, there seem to be too many contentious issues that degrade the relations: charges of espionage, campaign donations, human rights violations, nuclear proliferation, WTO membership: from ideological to economic to military, you name it; it's not a pretty picture.

Into the middle of this ugly mess, three or four laser-guided 2000 lb. missiles have fallen from the sky. And the scorched bodies of three innocent journalists have risen from the ashes. What else do you need to sink the already strained relations to the lowest point in recent memory?

Was the anger shown by the Chinese protesters genuine? Which American would not be genuinely angry if an American embassy was bombed by another country? Still remember how genuinely outraged you were when the two U. S. embassies in Africa were bombed by terrorists? Shouldn't you be equally outraged—if not more so—when a country professes to be your friend, yet turns around and bombs the hell out of your embassy? Wouldn't you call that a heinous betrayal? Then, it's not so hard to see why the Chinese—students, teachers, shop owners, government workers, the educated (with access to Voice of America, BBC, or the Internet, notwithstanding) and the uneducated alike—could not help but be shocked.

The images that flashed across the minds of many Chinese were of opium, gunboats, palaces being burnt down, and "Chinese and Dogs Are Not Allowed In" signs in our own parks. To many of them, it's the latest evidence of how the U.S.-led West would like to treat China. Its intentions seem far from benign.

Call it xenophobia if you may, but this fear and hatred, and the prevalent sense of victimization is not only the product of paranoiac imaginations. Americans, on the other hand, do not have the experience of fighting a foreign aggressor on their own soil, though many times they have had to send their boys outside the borders to fight for justice, territorial expansion and other stated or unstated goals. To many of them, the Chinese reaction is more than puzzling.

Was the rage orchestrated? Very likely. The Chinese leaders themselves, like the average Chinese, must have been genuinely shocked and outraged. If they had not endorsed the students and other protesters, the rage could have turned in other directions, most likely towards them for being passive or appearing weak.

Their ambitious economic reforms have produced, among other things, widespread discontent. Appearing weak at such a time would certainly not work to their advantage. Endorsing the protest also would serve to divert attention from the upcoming 10th Anniversary of Tiananmen Square. So the decision was not too difficult to make. Yet, you could not accuse them of having orchestrated something along the lines of "Wag The Dog."

Was it excessive? It depends on who you are. The besieging of the American embassy and consulates, and attacking them with such projectiles as eggs, rocks, etc., shows once again how easily any such large demonstrations (including the anti-war protests in this country in the 60s, and the democracy movement in China in 1989) can get out of hand and become riotous.

The U.S.-led West did not help defuse the explosive situation with their flip-flop explanations (CIA and outdated maps?) either. How would you explain such "collateral damage" to the family members of the three journalists? Clinton's repeated apologies don't carry much weight since, at the moment, he has a major credibility problem. And the apologies were withheld for two days by the government-controlled media in China towards an obvious calculated effect.

For their part, many Chinese fail to see that you have to be really cynical to believe that the bombing was intentional. NATO and its highest command would have to have been out of their minds to deliberately target the embassy of a permanent member of the UN Security Council when it needed the cooperation of that country the most. It would have been a

Frailty, Thy Name is—

bullheaded defiance of simple logic, basic decency, and a flagrant betrayal of every humanitarian ideal the West has professed to uphold. They could not appreciate the fact that the U. S. feels that, as the only remaining superpower in the world today, it has a moral obligation to intervene when large-scale humanitarian disasters are happening. Especially when footage of devastated refugees bombards your TV screen every day for so long. The U. S. always plays watchdog more eagerly when its own vital interests are at stake, which may explain why it did not intervene as aggressively elsewhere when equally, if not more, disastrous atrocities were being committed.

If any hypocrisy or double standard is involved here, it is within reasonable bounds. And for such an oft-thankless role, Americans have put their young men and women in harm's way. The price they pay is huge, in terms of tax dollars, emotional and moral agony and tragedy, and human lives.

So, the two countries should again look at the big picture. They should stop sensationalizing the differences irresponsibly, quit calling each other names (such as hypocrites) and pointing fingers at each other in juvenile fashion, and start repairing the damage that has been done. As any Chinese and American with common sense and average intelligence should know, a healthy, mature and stable relationship between the two countries is too important (not only to themselves, but also to the world at large) to be sacrificed at the altar of this unfortunate and tragic turn of events.

Dance with Chains

Deng's Epic

FEBRUARY 26, 1997

IT WAS ABOUT 2:45 IN THE AFTERNOON. I was adding another topic to the instructions for the first position paper in a literature course I was teaching this spring: How can William Blake's poem "The Chimney Sweeper"(1789) yield two opposite interpretations?

The phone rang. It was a friend of mine: "Deng Xiaoping has died," he said.

So it has happened, at last.

I turned off the computer, went downstairs, turned on the TV, and switched to the channel of a Chinese news network, headquartered in Taiwan. It runs around the clock in the fashion of CNN.

There he was, smiling at me from a picture (taken probably in his 80's) framed with wide dark strips. Notes from a low, mournful dirge began to fill the air of the sitting room. Then, there was the replay of the announcement read by a China Central TV anchor, dressed in a dark suit. He delivered the words in a painfully slow and solemn voice.

I searched in my heart to assess the impact of the sudden news: no overwhelming feeling of denial, sadness, despair or joy. What I was experiencing was a calm acceptance of the inevitable, and resignation to yet further, incontrovertible proof that human life is frail.

This, I soon found out, was also the emotional response of several of my Chinese friends here. I can bet that it was echoed widely among the more than one billion Chinese in the world.

Back in 1976, on a sunny September afternoon, I was "re-educating" myself by hoeing a vegetable field with some peasants when the loudspeaker announced the death of Mao

Zedong. All of a sudden, the earth shook and the sky came crashing down. Tears, uncontrollable, hysterical tears welled up from the bottoms of millions of hearts, and flooded the shameless slopes of millions of cheeks.

This drastic difference in reaction is significant: it signifies that China, though one of the oldest countries in the world, has finally grown up. And Deng himself has much to do with this.

In 1920, at the age of 16, Deng left his small hometown in central China for France, to look for a panacea for the ills of the most plagued giant in the Orient. While in Europe, along with other young expatriate idealists such as Zhou Enlai, Deng found Marxism, took it home, and began to apply it to his motherland. The rest, as people on this side of the Pacific would say, is history.

But how to evaluate Deng's role in Chinese history?

Many would praise Deng as one of the greatest leaders in modern Chinese history, or of the 20th century, for that matter. Counted among his achievements would be: the normalization of relations with the former Soviet Union; the opening up and reforming of China, both of which have led to its miraculous economic development; the visionary "One Country, Two Systems" concept which has laid the groundwork for the smooth transfer of power of Hong Kong this year, and possibly for the peaceful reunification with Taiwan in the future. Quite an impressive list.

His detractors would denounce him as the last new emperor of China, who ruled China with an iron hand, and with as much trickery and ruthlessness as Mao before him. Topping the list of his crimes would be his ordering tanks to run down students on the Tiananmen Square in 1989.

Indeed, Deng's life, from boarding the ship to France, through the death-ridden Long March, through all the precarious ups and precipitant downs in his political fortune, until breathing his last on February 19, is an epic that can yield much more divergent interpretations than Blake's poem.

I'm not an historian, and even historians need considerable temporal distance to reach any definitive evaluation of Deng's place in history. Even when time affords such perspective, historians are bound to disagree.

Again, a comparison of Mao and Deng may be a useful gauge here.

When the semi-god Mao died, he left behind economic and political ruin, resulting from his paranoiac obsession with ideological fights.

Deng's Epic

It's true that today's China has achieved far less than the Utopia Deng dreamed of as a youth: the widening gap between the rich and the poor, rampant corruption, environmental crises—the list goes on and on.

But the earthly Deng left China with the kind of prosperity that would have been inconceivable only a few years ago. Politically, the country is stable, and the power structure is as benign and quiet as it ever has been.

Yes, Deng is also largely responsible for delaying political reforms. What was he thinking when he ordered the pulling down of "democracy walls" in Beijing of the early 1980s? What was on his mind when he ordered the bloody and tragic crackdown in June of 1989? Had he become the infallible "Son of the Heaven" in his own eyes, or did he act out of his staunch faith in Communism: a faith he felt was being challenged by the democracy movement?

One thing is certain: Deng was only human, and to be human is to err. Deng was also Chinese, and being Chinese, he could not transcend the over four thousand years of Chinese civilization with all its burdensome heritages. He did what he did, for better or for worse, not only because who and what he was, but also in spite of who and what he was.

To gloss over his fatal errors and idolize him would be foolish. To heap all the blame for China's problems on his head would betray a juvenile lack of historical perspective.

To be overjoyed at the death of a 92-year-old man, as a few fanatical expatriate political activists have done, would only reveal a loss of one's basic humanness.

In his will, Deng instructed to have his retina donated to the blind, his other organs to medical research, and his ashes spread into the China seas. For this alone, I will salute in his direction.

Deng has died. The sky has not fallen. The era of strong man politics in China is over. It's not improbable that from the current collective leadership will eventually evolve a more democratic system of government in China. A stable, prosperous and democratic China is good for its own people and for the people of the rest of the world.

I remain cautiously optimistic.

Encouraging Signs

MAY 23, 1997

THE COMING CONFLICT WITH CHINA (1997) by Richard Bernstein and Ross H. Munro is being promoted as an "informed and illuminating" study of a possible "high-stakes clash" between the United States and China early next century due to competing ideologies and economic interests.

At the end of the book, the authors state that "it is not in the American interest to be an enemy of China." They express hope that a new generation of leaders, "more open-minded and tolerant, less reflexively defensive and chauvinistic," may eventually take over, and run China in a more democratic way. Thus, one of the great tasks of American diplomacy will be "to remain on good terms with the more cosmopolitan and liberal segments of the vast Chinese nation." "The surest way to avert the conflict with China," the authors conclude, "would be for that strain in Chinese life to triumph and to guide China as a whole into the twenty-first century."

While this somewhat upbeat conclusion hints at a thread of hope, the overall horizon projected by the book is depressing, and the policies recommended may serve to alienate—if not outright antagonize—this upcoming generation of Chinese.

Most of this generation, whether schooled in American and European universities, or at home, would agree with the authors that there has been a lot of repression in the political life in China. One of the most tragic emblems of that repression was the bloody crackdown on the Tiananmen Square. Political reforms have been dragging behind economic reforms which have led to the current boom. But they also believe that democracy will eventually come to China.

Democracy has been dragging its feet in China because, since time immemorial, China has been governed by the Confucian ideal of social hierarchy. In that hierarchy, emperors rule with a "mandate from heaven," rather than the consent of the governed.

Encouraging Signs

From a social development point of view, since a huge percentage of Chinese today are still struggling at the subsistence strata of Maslow's hierarchy of human needs, opportunities for civil participation and social self-actualization are luxuries which only a small portion of the population either demands, or is ready to enjoy. It would be quite an exercise in futility and arbitrariness if 1.2 billion Chinese, literate or illiterate, informed or confused, woke up one Tuesday morning, swarmed to the polls and voted for the next president of the country. There would certainly be more and worse scandals than Watergate and the Lincoln Bedroom.

But there are encouraging signs. Since reforms began almost 20 years ago, living standards have improved dramatically, and a sizeable middle-class has emerged. Even though there is still almost paranoiac ideological control of public forums, people in general are much freer than ever before, and can say virtually whatever is on their minds in non-public settings.

The judicial system has yet to develop into an independent arm of government, but laws concerning all aspects of life are being developed. Reforms to bring laws up to international norms have been introduced, and there are more and more cases of common citizens, armed with these new laws, suing government bureaucrats, and winning.

Moreover, people's congress at different levels is acquiring more political and policy-making power. In a recent session of the National People's Congress, several government motions and reports were accepted only after encountering more than 30% delegates voting nay, an unmistakable sign that the legislative body is seeking a more active role, rather than playing the rubber stamp and applauding unanimously whenever it is expected to.

The most promising of all are experiments with democracy at the grass-roots level in villages and townships where they are holding direct and open elections. There is a good possibility that such democratization will gradually work its way upward and change the whole political process—all in due time.

Chinese people, having suffered too much turmoil for too long, are tired of revolutions and bloodshed. They want to live a stable and prosperous life. They want democracy, but through gradual and peaceful evolution.

Besides, democracy is not an end in itself, but a means: a process whereby the Chinese may govern effectively, and ensure the largest amount of happiness for the largest number of people. To transplant full-blown, Western-style democracy into Chinese soil would probably not work. The Chinese people have to search and find a form of democracy that will best suit their own needs. All this takes time.

What role should the West play in this gradual process? At the very least, they should not pull at the seedling too aggressively in hopes of accelerating its growth. This has been tried, and has historically only worked to stunt growth, or destroy what it hopes to foster.

The policies recommended by Bernstein and Munro are just doing that.

The authors' main concerns are that the rise of China economically and militarily will upset "the balance of power" in Asia, and eventually threaten the "vital interests" of the United States. In order to prevent that from happening, they propose, among other things, suspending MFN, blocking China's WTO membership, rearming Japan, conducting joint military exercises in Southeast Asia and continuing to sell high-tech weaponry to Taiwan.

Such policies, however, only lend tangible evidence to the "Strangling China" conspiracy theory drummed up by Chinese leadership and state-controlled media.

It's true that in recent years, China has been more than eager to show off its newly acquired military prowess, but its strategic planning is defensive in nature and its precarious security environment—sharing borders with 14 countries with many unresolved territorial disputes—calls for a military power base commensurate to its size. Indeed, by the authors' own accounts, China, unlike the former Soviet Union, is not a "territorially and ideologically expansionist country with a rigidly controlled economy and a messianic, world-conquering vision of itself." It "has no intention of sending its troops to conquer the territory of other Asian countries."

Therefore, even "the more cosmopolitan and liberal" among the Chinese would be baffled why China could not develop its economy and military, and play a role in its region and the world comparable to its size? Why is a modern and strong China necessarily a threat to others?

As the authors note it, there is a tremendous amount of goodwill among the Chinese people toward the United States, which, in its Chinese translation, means "Beautiful Country." The implementation of their proposed policies would be a huge step backwards in relations. It could, very quickly, lead to another Cold War or arms race. More importantly, it might also cause a change of heart among the Chinese people. It could even cause the "more open-minded and tolerant," upcoming generation to be disillusioned and suspicious, hence, forfeiting the "surest" insurance policy against a catastrophic head-on collision. The about-face turn of the young authors of the sensational *China Can Say No* (1996), from pro-democracy to anti-American serves as a fresh example.

This would not be in the best interest of either the United States or China. Enough damage has been done to U.S.-China relations by cheap, juvenile and frenzied demonization on both sides. It's time for the two countries to act more maturely and responsibly for their own long-term interest.

It may be true that it is difficult for superpowers to be lovers. However, at the very least, they should be able to find ways to be peaceful neighbors and even partners. You'd think we would have learned something and gained some wisdom from the past. Sometimes I wonder.

Hong Kong at Sunrise

JUNE 30, 1997

THE COUNTDOWN IS FAST APPROACHING: midnight, June 30th, 1997.

At this historical moment, to be watched by the whole world, the sun will set forever for the British Empire in the Far East, and the Five-Starred Red Flag will replace the tri-colored Union Jack. The latter is nicknamed the "Rice Flag" in China because of its design which resembles the Chinese character for that ubiquitous grain.

But it was not the white, sweet and nutritional grain that ships flying the flag with the crosses of the three patron saints were carrying to China in the early 1800s. The British loved Chinese tea, its elegant silk, and exquisite porcelain. Their merchants, however, were not willing to spend silver to bring these fine goods home. Endowed with sharp business acumen, they paid instead with a dark brown, highly addictive narcotic powder, refined from a plant called poppy (*Papaver*) grown in India, a British colony then.

The opium trade did so well that, in the years 1835-6, the total amount of the narcotic brought to China rose to 27,111 chests (almost 4 million pounds) valued at $17,904,248. By 1838, in the southeastern Fujian and Guangdong provinces, 90% of the population had become miserable opium addicts. Naturally, even the muddleheaded Emperor in Beijing became alarmed. A decree was issued, opium was confiscated and burned along the coast, or flushed into the sea. Fleets of steam-driven gunships were sent across the oceans, and the tiny island of Hong Kong was taken by the red-coated soldiers of Her Majesty. This was the infamous Opium War of 1839-1842.

Soon afterward, the neighboring Kowloon peninsula was occupied, too, and in 1898, a 99-year lease of the New Territories was extorted from China. These three parts form what is now generally known as Hong Kong.

Apologists for the opium traders have argued that China got what it deserved because it refused to open up to international trade. What would these same pious, free-trade believers have to say, conscionably, to today's drug traffickers? Or to the commandos parachuting into Panama to hustle Noriega out of hiding, and drag him before a grand jury in the U.S.?

The opium trade was indisputably, as some historians have put it, "the most unsavory and ignoble episode in British mercantile ventures, surpassed only by the horrors of the slave trade."

Hong Kong's return has to be viewed in this historical perspective.

And the return was not initiated by the United Kingdom because it suddenly felt guilt-stricken and decided, out of the goodness of its heart, to relinquish what rightfully belonged to China. Indeed, when Margaret Thatcher was in Beijing in the fall of 1982, she was still jabbering about the legitimacy of British occupation of the island of Hong Kong and the Kowloon peninsula although the New Territories would be returned when the "lease" expired in 1997.

But it was not a sickly, sleeping giant that the "Iron Lady" was talking to. Thus began the serious negotiation of returning the whole of Hong Kong to Chinese sovereignty after 156 years of British rule.

Although the majority of people in Hong Kong welcome the historical return, there is a lot of nostalgia. After all, having lived under the British rule for generations, the Chinese in Hong Kong have become used to the Union Jack flying in the sky, Her

Majesty's profile gracing the coins and bankrolls, and the melody of "God Saves the Queen." Witness how hard it is for the Britons to vote the scandal-plagued Royalty out of service: they love the pomp in front of Buckingham Palace so much.

There is a considerable amount of anxiety, too. And with good reason. While a historical transition of such a magnitude would inevitably encounter some friction, the Chinese government may have invited much of this upon itself, noticeably, by its crackdown at Tiananmen Square, and its recent attempts to roll back some of the civil liberties gained by the Hong Kong inhabitants since the early 1990s.

It is true that Hong Kong's inhabitants have enjoyed meager civil rights despite the *laissez-faire* economic system and rule of law. They have often been treated as second-class citizens in their own land. There were basically no democratic processes, and the governor appointed by the monarch could follow his own whims running the colony without any real checks or balances.

It is also common sense that during the transitional period, stability should be one of the highest priorities to ensure Hong Kong's continued prosperity. Even limiting foreign contributions to political organizations in Hong Kong would be understandable, considering that democracies like the United States have set such precedents. This is not to suggest that political demonstrations or public speeches should be curtailed or censored in any way since that would only lead to an erosion of public confidence and to social instability.

Looking at its past, the Chinese leadership has come a long way in setting up the "One Country, Two Systems" structure, and in developing the "Basic Law" whereby Hong Kong is to be governed. Yet, if it genuinely believes that it represents the best interests of the majority of the people, and enjoys their full support, then it should also trust that they in return will exercise their civil liberties responsibly. It should at least develop some healthy sense of humor, feeling flattered even by unflattering cartoons or burning of effigies. A ready role model would be the Clintons, who laughed heartily with Don Imus when he told off-color jokes at their expense right in their face, and in the full glare of the TV camera. The bottom line should take heed the Chinese axiom: let the people speak and the sky will not fall.

This blunder aside, however, China should be credited for appreciating fully the incalculable importance of Hong Kong to the mainland, to Taiwan and to all interested foreign countries, and for having acted accordingly.

All signs counted, July 1, 1997 will not be the doomsday of Hong Kong, as a few hysterical alarmists have announced, and the golden goose will not be killed.

At sunrise on that day, and for a long time to come, Hong Kong will remain the Fragrant Harbor, as its name (derived from the sweet-smelling incense trees found there) in Chinese signifies.

China's Gamble

SEPTEMBER 22, 1997

THE TOP FLOOR OF A GIRLS' SCHOOL in the French Concession—one of those odd entities in China then, a virtual sovereignty within another sovereign country—in Shanghai. A conclave of 13 twentysomethings was in progress. Sighting suspicious visitors (were they government agents?) snooping around outside, they relocated, and resumed their meetings on a small boat in another province.

It was a time during which the once-proud Giant of the Orient had been continuously forced to her knees for well over half a century: when numerous unequal treaties had been forced down her throat, literally at gunpoint, and when the country was being plagued by warlordism, poverty and despair. It was a country Teddy Roosevelt held much in contempt because a short while before, she had been defeated shamefully by a much smaller island country from whence the sun is purported to rise, and because her people hopelessly lacked a passionate national spirit.

It was a country Woodrow Wilson, though sympathetic, had just found it convenient to yield up to Japan and its 21 Demands (essentially to annex a big part of Northeastern China) at the Paris Conference where prizes and trophies for the winners of the Great World War were being divided.

Though claiming a population of 400 million, the most populous in the world then, China had suffered one devastating defeat after another in the hands of foreign powers. A tragic sense of despair was dominant among the young and the intellectuals at the time. By all signs, the Chinese civilization, very much an endangered species, was doomed to extinction.

China's Gamble

It was at this time of crisis that the 13 met: one of them, a youth called Mao, from central China. They were worried. They were disappointed with the slew of monarchical reforms that had been enacted, and disillusioned with the recent victory of the republican revolution. They eagerly leafed through the pages of *Das Kapital* and *Communist Manifesto* written by a big-bearded German. And they thought they had found the panacea for their sickly motherland. Armed with half-digested theories of surplus value, economic determinism, and class struggle, they set out not only to save and modernize their motherland, but also to turn it into a communist utopia.

That was July, 1921.

Perhaps, it was the inauspicious number of delegates for the first congress of the Chinese Communist Party. Though the spark soon spread like wildfire, it was all but extinguished in the coming years. The CCP, with its tiny, ill-equipped guerrilla army, was dismissed by the outside world as bandits under the red cover of Communism, much like the authenticity of the Christian uprising of the Heavenly Peace—led by Hong Xiuquang—was suspected half a century before. Indeed, the "red bandits" were hunted down by government troops across thousands of miles of snow-capped mountains, treacherous swamps and severe wilderness.

They started the Long March with 100,000 men and women, and ended a year later with a meager 9,000. The rest had either been killed, had died of hunger, sickness or battle wounds, or had defected.

Somehow, their cause was reanimated during the War of Resistance Against Japan. Somehow, it inexorably won the hearts of the Chinese people, and somehow they all but wiped out the U.S.-financed and -equipped government troops. One morning in 1949, the world woke up and found that the most populous country on earth had fallen into the hands of the Communists.

Yet Communist victory did not deliver all it had promised. Yes, the country had finally stood up, won its independence and rid itself of many problems. Nevertheless, China was still in deep trouble.

The Chinese had to contend with many concurrent, and often contrary notions. There was the CCP's feverish idealism and its rigid ideology, and there was also the emperor mentality that had all but deified Mao. Add in the millennia of feudalistic and Confucian heritages, and a mostly backward, agrarian economy, and you have all the necessary ingredients to cook up some of the most catastrophic tragedies in its modern history. First, there was the Anti-Rightist Movement in the 50s, then the Cultural Revolution in the 60s, and—still fresh in our memory—the tragic crackdown on the Tiananmen Square in the summer of 1989. The CCP had stumbled over and again, failing miserably in the daunting task of juggling its monolithic ideology, its ambitious developmental objectives and the country's deep-rooted cultural traditions. The price they have paid is counted in the lives of the millions of people who perished.

So what has been going on in Beijing this past week? The meeting of the CCP's 15th National Congress may be regarded as a continuation of a second revolution started by Deng Xiaoping, a Long Marcher himself, to jumpstart the country's modernization by downplaying ideology. Since the end of 1970s, especially during the last few years, China's economy has been experiencing explosive growth. At this meeting, President Jiang Zemin, long regarded a political lightweight, decided to make one bold move: to privatize (to varying degrees and in various forms) two-thirds of the state-run enterprises which have soaked up 90% of the available financial resources, but yielded only one third of the total industrial output. Of course, the state will retain ownership of the strategically important industries.

This is both an economic and a political gamble for the CCP because about 110 million workers will be affected when they are cut loose in the "sink or swim" currents of the market. Many of them will become unemployed, or underemployed.

Politically, if the economic reform fails, the CCP will lose big time because the social and economic basis of its leadership will be shaken. If the reform succeeds, the CCP will lose, too because, ironically, according to the classic Marxist theory, prosperity will naturally lead to demand for more active participation in the political process and decentralization, and privatization will inevitably threaten the CCP's power monopoly.

Will the CCP itself be reformed out of relevance? We don't know for sure. But one thing seems clear: it is clear-headed, and its success so far has given it confidence. The Party's grand plan is to achieve complete modernization by the end of the next century. To do so, it will downsize the armed forces by another half a million in the next three years (after a whole million was cut in the mid-1980s).

China's Gamble

Noticeably absent in this grand plan is significant political reform, but there are clear signs that the country is opening up in almost every other aspect of its life. Even this CCP meeting was much more open: multiple candidates, much more press access (including over one thousand journalists from outside China), and more airing of diverse views from the delegates.

The fact is, of the CCP's current 58 million cardholding membership, almost none has had to survive living on tree bark or wild weeds as their revolutionary fathers did during the Long March of the mid-1930s. And its top leadership is gradually becoming a governing body of technocrats, bureaucrats and administrators, instead of Communist idealists or ideologues.

While China is engaged in a Herculean economic reform, politically it might experience a slow free fall as the country's history unfolds itself and seeks its own logic at its own velocity. Will it take the whole world along with it? Where will it be 100 years from now?

The Albatross Over the Square

June 4, 1999

Fire, fire, everywhere.

Thousands upon thousands of young college students were demonstrating on this well-known, expansive square in the capital of China. Then, their anger and frustration could not contain itself any more. They turned and marched toward the Legation Quarter—an extraterritorial district where representatives of Western Powers resided. Then, they marched toward the homes of the warlord government's leaders. They were joined by citizens from all walks of life, breaking through violent blockades set up by nervous police forces. They jumped over the fences, dragging those hated Chinese officials out of hiding. They beat them up, and set fire to their homes. During those agitated skirmishes, many were injured, arrested, thrown into jail...

This was not a scene from Tiananmen Square in 1989. It occurred 80 springs and autumns ago. The most feverish episode of this student movement lasted from May 4 until June 4, 1919.

If the students were disgusted with the Western Powers, who used WW1's Paris Peace Conference to levy all kinds of injustices against the Chinese, they were much more incensed by the corruption that plagued this once proud giant in the Orient. To them and their professors—new intellectuals who had just returned from studies abroad—the only way to save China was to rid herself of the stifling Confucian traditions, and inject into her system the revolutionary Western concepts of Democracy and Science. This intellectual revolution, which spanned several years and rocked the very foundations—cultural, as well as sociopolitical—of the Central Kingdom, left a lasting impact on the course of modern China. One offshoot was of course, the Chinese Communist Party (CCP) itself.

Tiananmen was built in 1417. With its crimson color, and colossal, majestic presence is, literally and figuratively, the heart of Beijing. It means "Heavenly Peace Gate" in Chinese, but it has rarely seen peace since that May in 1919. It would bear witness to numerous demonstrations during the War of Resistance Against Japan (1937-1945), and the ensuing Civil War (1945-49). Out of both despair and hope, students along with teachers, workers, and shop owners marched down the same square again and again under the same banners of freedom, democracy, peace and sovereignty. Many such demonstrations ended in arrests, injuries, and deaths.

During the peak of the Cultural Revolution (1966-1976), Mao emerged from behind the scenes on top of the Tiananmen, and inspected his troops: an ocean of frenzied and adoring young Red Guards. They waved the little red book, they danced, sang and screamed revolutionary hymns. Tears of rapture washed down their cheeks. Mao was to emerge atop this Gate of Heavenly Peace eight times, altogether: either to push the revolution to its logical end as he perceived it, or to consolidate his grip on power.

This 10-year nightmare all but paralyzed the most populous country in the world, robbing youths of their dreams, turning humans into beasts, ending the lives of innocent people, ruining families too numerous to count and leaving scars too deep to be completely healed even now.

Fire, fire, everywhere.

The scenes from the same square exactly ten years ago today are too painful and too recent to recount here. The tragic irony of it all is that the CCP, itself being a child of a movement calling for Mr. Democracy and Mr. Science, sent tanks and troops to crack down another generation of young college students thirsting for the same things. It authored one of the darkest pages in Chinese history.

Tiananmen in 1989 started as a protest of living conditions: the food served in student cafeterias, among other things. Quickly, it changed into a battle cry against corruption in the government at various levels. Soon, it expanded into a political movement, demanding faster and broader political reforms, which would give the citizens more civil and political liberties.

Paradoxically, the CCP was a victim of its own policies to open up China and to engage in economic reforms. At one point during the chaos, the CCP's power base was rendered precarious.

What are the legacies of Tiananmen Square?

While the government has been choreographing its months-long celebrations commemorating the 80th anniversary of the earlier movement, it has kept sheepishly quiet on the 10th anniversary of the more recent one.

Nevertheless, the Albatross hangs from the neck of the CCP and the Central Government. Their image is irrevocably tarnished. No matter what it enacts now, whatever policies it forwards, domestic or international, every move is looked upon through the eerily, crimson smoke and fire burning on the square in the early hours of June 4, 1989. Even its support of the recent student demonstrations, protesting the bombing of the Chinese embassy in Yugoslavia was thus scrutinized.

Does it matter that many of the young students didn't really understand what democracy really meant and that some became riotous? Does it matter that the crackdown order was given in a rather precarious moment during the sociopolitical life of China (on the verge of anarchy largely due to the government's refusal to really listen to the students), and in the world at large?

Ten years may be no more than a tiny ripple in the endless river of history. It should, however, provide a historical perspective long enough to set straight the records, to own up the tragic blunder and to begin the healing process.

To prevent such tragedies from ever happening again, the government should push more wholeheartedly for more substantial political reforms so that the rule of law and a healthy system of justice, checks and balances, which fits China the most, can be established. All of this must be done, in spite of the real risk that the CCP itself might eventually be reformed out of its monopoly of power.

The Albatross will not fall from around its neck until the ghosts of the wronged are appeased.

In the early days of the CCP, a youthful Mao prophesied that a little spark could well start a wildfire that would spread far and wide. Will a China, closer to the ideals envisioned by the May Fourth Youths some 80 years ago, emerge from the fire of Democracy that has been raging in this ancient country ever since?

China At Crossroads

OCTOBER 3, 1999

I WASN'T THERE ON OCTOBER 1, 1949, when Mao emerged on the rostrum of the Tiananmen Square to proclaim in his heavy Hunan accent that "The Chinese people have stood up," though the proclamation was heard around the world and sent chills down the spines of many in Washington who would run around and accuse each other of having "lost" China.

I also missed the Korean War which threatened the very being of the young People's Republic right after its birth. I was destined, however, not to miss any single, earth-shaking event that has happened since the spring of 1957. That was the year Mao, after flirting with "The Hundred Flower Movement," (which promised more freedom of speech and artistic expression) changed his mind, and swept out all of those thousands of outspoken intellectuals, calling them "poisonous weeds." They were banished to labor camps and out-of-the-way areas to languish—until the Cultural Revolution. Then, their situation got worse.

In the late 1950s, the People's Republic was caught in a fever called "Communist Wind," which was supposed to launch China into an orbit whereby it would overtake England and the U.S. in years that could be counted on fingers. Pots and pans were smashed to make steel on the village square, astronomical figures of production goals were announced and soil was ploughed three feet deep to ensure bumper harvests. The result was disastrous.

Even today, I still have a below average stature to testify to the hunger and stunted growth I suffered during the subsequent "Three Years of Natural Disasters," so dubbed officially, though in reality, it was a tragedy of human folly. When the fever was gone, millions had lost their lives.

My memories of the Cultural Revolution were the clearest and most painful, though. As a young school boy I witnessed my dear father being locked up in a dark room, tortured and paraded along streets. I was forced to denounce him as a capitalist-roader and anti-revolutionary. I refused and was harassed for my stubborn loyalty. When that nightmare was over ten years later, my father had lost his prime years and his health. His hair was gray. Thousands, if not millions, of others did not even survive the ordeal.

More things have happened since then. More tragedies. More lost lives. So, as the spectacular fireworks are illuminating the skies on the other side of the Pacific to mark the 50th anniversary of the People's Republic, I ask myself: Is there much to celebrate?

The answer should be an unequivocal "yes." The People's Republic has not delivered everything it promised. It has stumbled and made catastrophic missteps, but the Chinese people have indeed stood up. They have earned the right to stand tall, to be respected and not to be trifled with.

In terms of sheer production capabilities alone in numerous categories, China today is dozens and even hundreds of times more powerful than it was 50 years ago. At least, Chinese children today eat much better food, and are growing much taller. Most of them have no recollection of hunger. The achievements are truly phenomenal.

Nevertheless, the People's Republic is also steeped in crises. It is facing colossal challenges spiritually, politically and economically. Communism today is no more than a token faith for the majority of its 60 million strong members, the early idealistic fervor having been drastically chilled by sad failures at home and abroad.

Will the native Confucianism, Daoism, and Buddhism fill the void? Can patriotism or nationalism unite the 1.3 billion individuals who are bent on chasing their own stars and dreams? What about the recently outlawed Falun Gong that had promised everything from good health to immortality? Then, there are the foreign-looking evangelists who flock in to save souls and hand out Deliverance. Where is all this confusion and frenzied searching going to lead China?

If a country the size of China needs a strong spiritual bond to hold itself together, it cannot do so without a strong and stable political structure. Has the centralized, one-party rule outlived its relevance? If the answer is yes, as many would vehemently argue, what shall we do? Abolish the whole thing, and start all over? Replace it with an Euro-American style democracy? Or reform it from within to make it more just, fair and efficient? Only the naïve and ignorant could say the choice is an easy one.

The grass-roots experiments with democracy have been

encouraging. But will the efforts eventually turn the country into a mature democracy that fits by serving its people's best interests?

China's economic challenges are just as formidable: the worsening environment, the widening gap between rich and poor, between coastal and inland provinces, the treacherous state-owned enterprises reforms, rampant corruption, ever increasing un- and under-employment, the list goes on and on.

Looking beyond its borders, the People's Republic is facing a grim security environment. While it has all but resolved its disputes with northern neighbors formerly of the Soviet Union, thorny issues with several others remain.

Its ongoing quarrel with Taiwan only adds more explosiveness to the situation. Entangled in the midst of all this is the United States, the undisputed sole superpower in the world today. It does not know for sure how to deal with the up-and-coming power player. China is in an unenviable dilemma where if it does not seek to strengthen itself, it will be brushed off with contempt, and if it does, it will be condemned as menacing and threatening to others. An equilibrium is hard to find.

Is the forecast for China a bleak one?

There is no denying that China is facing crises. But which country in the world today isn't? As many know, the Chinese equivalent for crisis is both "danger" and "opportunity." A huge country with deep cultural roots, rich heritage and hard working people, China has survived challenges of comparable magnitude from both within and without, and has eventually thrived. Unsettling as they are, the challenges China faces today may translate into great opportunities. Along the way, however, the people may be forced to make agonizing choices that will have a wide impact and far-reaching repercussions.

Five decades have passed since the founding of the People's Republic. Its record in delivering on its promises leaves much to be desired. China is yet to catch up with England or the U.S. It will probably take another 50 years or so before its income per capita will be compared favorably with that of other industrialized nations.

On its fiftieth birthday, the People's Republic is at a crossroads, experiencing a profound change which may have no parallel in history. Tragedies similar to those mentioned earlier may repeat themselves down the road, but the country seems better equipped to handle the challenges than ever before. Herein lies hope.

Oh, that I could be here to see it fifty years from today.

Random Notes

THE FOLLOWING ARE CALLED RANDOM NOTES because they do not speak on the same subject and do not pretend to strike one uniform, thematic note. They only record a few observations I had during my four-week revisit to China in the summer of 1999.

"I Want a Bride!"

A MULTIMILLIONAIRE PLACED a full-page ad in the newspaper. He was looking for a bride who was young, pretty, fertile, endowed with all the virtues traditionally associated with Chinese womanhood, and above all, she must be college educated.

Obscenely rich, but never having been inside the walls of a college, the middle-aged divorcé was in dire need of someone who could bring youth, offspring and culture into his life. He was not shy in flaunting his European-style mansions, Mercedes-Benz, impressive investment portfolio and huge diamond rings (all of which he listed in the ad), but there was nothing he could do to pretend to be a man versed in classics. One can't buy an appreciation for music, painting or even fine dining. He constantly felt "the slings and arrows" of his more educated peers. They turned up their noses at him in spite of his money, and the meager salaries they were making. There seemed only one way to make up for the humbling deficiency: marriage. It never occurred to him to at least mention something about candlelight, moonlit walks on the beach, Tango, Mozart or Li Bai.

A marriage of money and culture? A graft of balding success with youthful beauty?

Within days, his "Bride Search Committee" received over 200 phone calls, from college students, schoolteachers, graduate students and one young woman from as far as England. All tolled, some 1,500 eager young women answered the ad, hoping to be the lucky one chosen to fill whatever void there was in the multimillionaire's life: enough women to start an all women's college. He had no reason to feel inferior to anyone on earth now.

Somewhere around this time, a 48-year-old woman also placed a personal ad in the newspaper. She was subtler than her aforementioned male counterpart, though. She mentioned mutual attractions, understanding, commitment to sharing life together, etc. Not a single response after a whole month had elapsed. Having lived the life of a divorcèe for ten years, she could not afford to lose any more time. So she decided to spice up the ad by adding the fact that she had been quite successful in business ventures, i.e., she was rich.

Almost instantly, her phone began to ring off the hook. Her beeper sang day and night, leaving her no peace. The first person to call was an excited, 19-year-old youngster. "I'm old enough to be your mother!" she reminded him, more annoyed than flattered.

"Age is no obstacle as long as you are rich," came the cool answer. Another young suitor told her much the same: "If you are as rich as you claimed in the ad, I would not hesitate at all to throw myself into your arms; your age is a non-issue to me."

When forced to tell the truth, a middle-aged suitor eventually had to admit that he was married, but that shouldn't stand between him and the rich woman, either: "Give me 50 thousand *yuan*, and I'll end my unfortunate marriage and tie the knot with you right away."

Another man, also obscenely rich and recently divorced, bragged, "With my fortune worth millions, I could find whatever woman I desired to be my wife, in no time." He went about hunting for a new bride with the same no-nonsense philosophy as he would a business deal: "delivery of goods upon payment." He would be turned down by one woman after another. The complaint? He didn't know how to love; he had no culture; and he was too bossy and manipulative.

Love is not a commodity after all? The jury is still out on this one.

A Visit to Hope's Home

GETTING OUT OF THE CAB—a small *Xiali* that could be seen running everywhere in my hometown Nanjing—I entered a long and deep alley. It was around 11:00 o'clock in the morning in the middle of July. Whatever early morning dew that moistened the face of a city as hot as Nanjing had long vanished. You could feel the heat surging up through the ground, and showering down from overhead. You were locked inside a sauna, and the key had been thrown away. Folks told me, though, that I was rather lucky, for this wasn't a bad summer at all. At least not as bad as the east coast back in the States which was being scorched by heat in the upper 90s for days on end.

The alley was throbbing with the hustle and bustle of everyday life, what with pedestrians hurrying to and fro, peddlers trying to sell their fresh produce and kids running around. Uncertain how deep the alley was, I stopped to ask passersby for directions several times. " Straight ahead. You won't miss it."

Finally, at a 90-degree right turn, I spotted on the left corner, a gate wide enough to allow two trucks to go in and come out abreast of each other. Three big signs hung perpendicular on the right, one of which read: Nanjing Municipal Charity Agency.

Brushing against the concrete structures of the gate was the rich foliage of sweet-scented osmanthus and plane trees. Excited, I took out the Sony Digital 8 from my bag, and began to shoot. I promised myself that I'd show the tape to Hope, who had called this place her home for as long as she could remember, until one morning she woke up and found that she had become a daughter of a happy American family somewhere in central Pennsylvania. Already 12 years old at the time of adoption, she had been dying for a family, a real family, as she later would describe at one of my weekend Chinese language classes. Her prayers had finally been answered.

I caught a middle-aged woman in the lens, who was coming out from inside of the gate, and brought her closer by pressing the "T" button. She saw me, looked puzzled and decided to walk in my direction. I turned off the camera.

"What's it you're doing?" No anger. All politeness. And alertness. In the back of my mind appeared a collage of pictures I had seen on the Net. Tiny, helpless babies. Bony. Skinny. Half-dead. And inflammatory charges and countercharges. I told her that I was on a mission here: I wanted to see people who had taken care of Hope. And her little friends. As a tangible proof of my good intentions, I showed her the gift pack prepared by Hope. Relieved visibly, she told me to go in, pointing at a building towards the back of the compound.

What caught my eye first was a statue, about two-stories high, right in the middle of the compound. It was a young female figure, wavy hair, shapely and curvy body, her head tilting heavenward. In her two hands, she held a white dove above her head, about to release the bird into the sky. Around her and at her waist were several angel-like young kids (orphans?), hands joined, the same heavenward gaze.

The foundation of the statue was a water fountain. Beyond that was a rather grassy and greenish, neatly-manicured lawn. The whole scene spoke of love, longing and dreams. Towering over the statue, further into the compound was the main building: seven-stories high, clean and still somewhat new. I could hear kids' voices floating out of the windows.

The hallways may not have earned the epithets of "sparkle and shine," but they were certainly spotless, having been mopped thoroughly either the night before or early that morning. They smelled of detergent.

Following the woman's instructions, I walked into the elevator, pushed the button, and in a few seconds, was on the fifth floor. I was told by a woman in a white uniform that the teacher I was looking for was off-duty that day. But she stopped whatever she was doing, and took me to the office of the head teacher of that floor. "Yes, I still remember her. Wei Hong, that's her Chinese name. How's she doing over there?" The head teacher was matronly and genuinely at peace with herself.

We walked down the hallway and came to the classroom where Wei Hong's (or Hope's) friends were. "You have a visitor from the U.S. He has brought you Wei Hong's greetings," the head teacher announced after pushing open the door.

The kids—more than a dozen of them—were watching TV (What else would you expect them to do on a hot, summer day?); they turned around, jumped out of their seats, stampeded towards us, and took the bag from my hand. They each found the card or letter addressed to themselves, which had taken their now-American friend more than a week to prepare, tore them open, and began to devour every word, loudly.

Two or three of the girls were, like Wei Hong, already in their early teens. Being too old for adoption, they'd perhaps call the orphanage their home all their life; they'd go to school, grow up, get a job and get married, all from here, as I had seen on China Central TV.

"Wei Hong was lucky," the head teacher said, matter-of-factly. There was a new law in place now. Anyone older than 10 would not be eligible for adoption.

Why had their parents abandoned them? I had no answers. Okay, I did see dullness in the eyes of some of the kids. Otherwise, they looked very normal to me.

In my mind's eye I could see another group of Chinese girls—between two to three years old—in central Pennsylvania. We had met several times already. In churches. At our celebrations of traditional Chinese holidays. Black hair. Yellow skin. Sparkling eyes. In the loving care of their new American parents. More than 70 such American families in this area alone. Some girls were still shy, having just arrived. Some were already speaking fluent American English. Wei Hong, or Hope, was the oldest of them all. At the local Chinese New Year's celebration in 1999, she went on the stage, and performed a Chinese folk dance with a group of other teenage girls. She has a large family now, her parents, Jim and Jennifer, a brother and two sisters.

"Can I videotape the classroom and the kids for Wei Hong?"

"Sure," came the answer from the head teacher. I could see excitement in her face, too. The wall on the right had a huge bulletin board filled with colorful drawings of trees, and human figures enjoying the cool shade under the trees. On the wall facing the door was a blackboard on which several poems were copied in chalk. One of them a classic by a well-known emperor-poet, venting his pensive thoughts on a moon-lit night about the evanescence of life. One was a parody of a popular song feigning a complaint about the never-ending homework assignment, the summer heat and life's other little annoyances.

Then, they began to line up in front of me. They wanted to talk to the camera, or rather, to Wei Hong, their American friend whom they had not seen for two years. They were a bit camera shy. A few had to be pushed to the camera by their peers, giggling. But their messages were warm and from the bottom of their hearts: study hard, make good progress, and above all, be happy.

Hadn't we—my wife and I, half-seriously and half-jokingly—talked about adopting a girl, having fallen in love with all the 70-some little Chinese (and more accurately, American) girls in central Pennsylvania?

We posed for pictures, me standing amongst them, awash in a feeling I had never known before. After bidding the kids farewell, I went to the central office with the head teacher, wrote a check there, and in the midst of the flurry, I forgot to ask about the procedures involved in adoption by Chinese natives living in the States.

I wondered what Hope would say when she saw the pictures and the videotape.

I Broke My Promise

"WHAT DO YOU THINK of the embassy bombing?" I had just sat down in the backseat of the car, and could now breathe with some ease. I was all dirty and sweaty from the transpacific flight, and the struggle to squeeze my two luggage bags into the awkward, user-unfriendly trunk of the Santana, a "sinicized" model resembling a VW. It was already past 8:30 on the evening of July 5th. The booming cosmopolitan city was churning out there, wide awake, restless and afire with rainbow neon lights.

Before getting off the Boeing 747 at the Shanghai International Airport, I had promised myself to keep my mouth shut about such sensitive topics. Yet, unable to resist the temptation of an eager audience, I opened my mouth at the very first opportunity to talk. Obsolete maps. Laser guided smart bombs. Razor sharp images from satellites. Breakdown in the chain of command and communications. Sheer stupidity, or incompetence. Conspiracies to derail the search for peaceful solutions in Kosovo and to sabotage U.S.—China relations. Biased reporting prior to and post embassy bombing. My narrative was punctuated with a few spirited Q&A, "Beg to differ," "See, I told you so," and nodding and shaking heads in a rather knowing way. Half way through with our climb up to the seventh floor of our destination, with one of the suitcases on my back, I was still talking.

I'd break my solemn promise again two days later when I arrived at my hometown, Nanjing. As our Chevy minivan was leaving the railway station near the star-lit Xuanwu Lake, the same question was posed to me. It was already 9 o'clock in the evening, I was still jet-legged, or sleep deprived, but I'd talk until I felt dizzy.

I'd be asked the same question many more times by friends, relatives, and old and new acquaintances. These folks were by no means conspiracy theory junkies, not by any stretch of the term. They had seen the photos of the three journalist-martyrs, and the smoldering and bomb-blasted building in Belgrade. They had heard a lot. The rallies. The funerals. The mournful music when the bodies of the martyrs were being carried off the plane in Beijing. They discussed the $4.5 million settlement, and how the money would be divided among the victims' families and more than a dozen other embassy personnel whose dreams had been blown to pieces on that most inauspicious night. They just wanted to know more. After all, NATO itself seemed not to be completely convinced of its own official explanation.

Later, I stumbled upon an on-line discussion, dealing with the subject of China's media coverage of the embassy bombing. It was organized by a magazine affiliated to the *People's Daily*: the mouthpiece of the Chinese Communist Party. One media specialist commented that the Chinese state-run media should have reported Clinton's apology immediately after he delivered it. Why? Because when they finally did carry the story, people with access to Hong Kong media (via satellite dish), and the Internet had been talking about it for more than two whole days, which made the state-run media look foolish and uninformed. What this scholar was not aware of, or did not care to point out, was that the belated coverage may have been caused by something other than a lack of sensitivity to newsworthiness.

The debris left by the bombing could still be seen. But certain things remain intact. Around the midnight the day before I was leaving, a relative of mine called. With a master's degree in sports psychology, and having worked in a provincial government agency for 10 years, he wanted to come to the States to pursue a doctoral degree in human development. Should I encourage him to pursue his dreams in America—the Beautiful

Country in Chinese translation—which would mean leaving behind his wife and his five-year-old, precocious son? Should I persuade him to stay and develop his potential in China? He already knew some professors in this field at Nanjing University, a Chinese Ivy League school ranked right after Peking and Qinghua Universities. I struggled, while lying in bed, not knowing what the best advice would be.

"Where Can We Go to Find Jobs, Sir?"

I WAS LOOKING OUTSIDE the window of the bus, my eyes feasting on a city that had changed so much since my last visit three years before. "Where can we go to find jobs, sir?" a throaty voice, in a thick dialect that I could not associate with a specific region, asked from behind my neck.

I turned around and faced a man in his forties, his hair cut almost to the scalp, his skin overly tanned, leathery, almost shiny, and his eyes a mixture of hope, confusion and stubbornness. "We're from the countryside and do not know where to go for jobs."

Jobs for whom? He turned around, and pointed to a gangly, tall youth sitting in a back seat. He could have been in his late teens. Perhaps he had just turned 20. He was clean and thin, and wore a homemade shirt, tucked into his homemade pants. An innocent country youth, free of irony or worldly sophistication. He was definitely not the typical city brat, the my-dad-makes-more-money, I-have-seen-it-all, don't-bother-me-because-I-don't-really-care sort of kid. "He has just earned a certificate for welding," his dad added.

A virtual outsider in my hometown, I turned to my cousin, who was sitting next to me, for help. Ten years my junior, and a savvy Net surfer, my cousin gave the middle-aged man a rather impatient look. He told the man to get off two more stops later, walk across a bridge, turn right, and walk another 200 yards. "There, you'll find the biggest job center in the whole province." After the father and son got off, and the bus pulled away, I turned back and caught a glance at the two of them, tramping under the hot sun.

In a minute or two we passed the bridge, and right after the bridge was a big crossroads. Would they get lost? Would the young man be able to find a job? Would he fall into a trap and lose his youthful innocence? Okay, unlike his Hawthornian counterparts, he was being chaperoned by his father, but the father himself was not much a guide when it came to the ways of the city. It all might prove too much for the country kid, after all.

The city was right in front of me. High-rises. Four-star and five-star hotels. Fancy restaurants. Expensive imported wine, cosmetics, and T-shirts. Mansions for single families. Apartment compounds where a single square meter would cost the average Chinese five or six months' earnings. Thousands of city residents either unemployed or without steady work. Thousands more, like the father and son, were pouring into the cities, looking for jobs. The glamorous, side-by-side with the not so glamorous. The gilded age has arrived in my hometown.

Father Touched My Forehead

THE OTHER DAY I went to the cemetery to pay a visit to my father. I had promised him that I'd come back to visit him more often than when I was a student. But three years had passed since my last visit. So I could not wait to visit him again.

It was a sweltering hot day. By the time we got to the cemetery, on the other side of the Yangtze, it was almost noon. Father gazed at me from his picture on the headstone with the same kindness I had known all my life. It had been four years since he passed away, and I was still struggling with the reality of his death.

The man who had given me my life was lying there, and would never wake up again. I stood in front of his picture, speechless. My mind went blank. All of a sudden, I felt something bursting in my heart and my cheeks were awash with tears.

That evening, I had a slight headache, and when I felt my forehead, it seemed somewhat warmer than usual. It was still early, but I was already sleepy. Thinking that I was just a bit tired and could simply sleep it off, I went to bed. The next morning, the headache and fever did not go away. At breakfast, I mentioned this to my mother. She thought for a moment, then said, "Maybe it's your father. He was happy to see you back, and touched your forehead to show his happiness."

Mother went to the kitchen, came back with a half dozen chopsticks, and a bowl of water. She explained, half apologetically, knowing that I don't believe in this sort of thing, "Let's see if it was really your father. I'm going to stick the heads of the chopsticks to the bottom of the bowl and then let go. If the chopsticks stand by themselves instead of falling, that would be a sign that you father did touch your forehead."

At that, she put the chopsticks in the bowl, and began to murmur something like: "If you did touch Shouhua's forehead because you were happy to see him, please answer me by remaining straight up." She let go, and the chopsticks stood there. Not one of them fell.

Had we really communicated with my father? I knew that we hadn't, but what if we had? That possibility, however slim it might be, brought tears to my eyes, and made me feel much better. That evening, my fever was gone.

So, what about the outlawed Falun Gong? An elixir (or snake oil) mixed with a bit of gong fu, a bit of religion, a bit of cult and a bit of superstition. Could it deliver what it had promised to his followers? I doubt it. Was it a ticking time bomb amid social stability? The way the state-run media had been bombarding the airwaves and front pages of newspapers with condemnations, it was. During the whole summer, the media was also full of admonitions to those who had been led astray, and to all citizens, as to how to adopt a politically correct and scientific attitude towards things of this nature.

I had no illusions about Falun Gong. I was convinced of the authenticity of the public repentance of some former Falun Gong followers, and the sad stories told by its victims. But isn't a nationwide campaign a bit too much? Is a tiny bit of superstition in our everyday life always a bad thing?

Have You Made Fortune Lately?

EVERYBODY IS AN INVESTOR nowadays. Everybody is talking about buying stock and selling stock. Fortunes have been made. Fortunes have been lost. In between, dreams are being realized, smashed or suspended somewhere in the limbo between the bid price and ask price. At least this is the impression I got during the summer.

"You guys in America are also playing stocks?" Friends would ask me, concerned that I would be left out of the game by staying in the States too long. Among the millions of dreamers who were anxious to hit the jackpot is a woman in her mid-60s, my step-mother-in-law: Han Mama.

A retired high school teacher, she has a modest retirement stipend. She wants her money to grow faster than the minuscule bank interest rate will allow her. She has heard too many stories of fortunes being made, literally overnight, by people she knows. So, she decided to join the club and play. To play, you have to register with an investment firm, so she registered with an investment firm on the other side of the town, which was quite inconvenient.

One morning, she left home right after breakfast. She was going to transfer her registration to another investment firm within walking distance of home. At around 10:30, she called home. She told me to look for her red purse. She remembered clearly that she had put it in her handbag before leaving. Now she was at the original investment firm but couldn't find the purse.

Following her instructions via cordless phone, I looked in the bedroom, inside her night table drawers, under her dresser and the dinner table. No. I couldn't find anything resembling her red purse. Then, it suddenly occurred to her that she may have lost the purse on the bus. The standing-room-only bus had moved in spastic fashion, throwing the passengers to and fro, left and right. A pregnant woman was standing very close behind her. In fact, she even remembered body contact. There were a few other passengers in close proximity, too. "Hold tight to me," mother-in-law told the pregnant woman, concerned that she would be thrown off balance and hurt.

That was the only chance somebody could have put his (or her) hand into the handbag. Pickpockets ganging up to prey on passengers, particularly older ones, is not unheard of on the buses there.

Her purse contained her ID, some cash and the investment registration card. Worried that the thieves could use the ID and the investment card to cause further damages, she called one of her daughters to come to her assistance right away. Yes, it was a desperate situation and it proved too much for her to handle all by herself. In her hurry to get to the investment firm, the daughter biked through a red light. She was detained by a cop, her bike was confiscated, at least for the time being, and she had to take a cab instead, to go to her mother's rescue.

In addition to the loss, mother-in-law would have to place a notice in the newspaper to nullify the stolen ID, and go to the public security office to get a temporary ID and apply for another permanent one, which would take at least six months to process. Then she would have to go back to the investment firm to finish the registration transfer with the temporary ID. To make matters worse, a few not so pleasant words were exchanged between her and father-in-law, thanks to the loss.

At the dinner table that evening, the old woman, totally exhausted, declared that she had lost her interest in "playing the stocks," for good.

PART III
A Happy Mean?

Blues, Fervor, and Stupidity

Election Year Blues on the Sidelines

MAY 6, 1996

IT'S ALL HER FAULT and I've repeatedly told her so.

It all started when Ms. Leona Baughman, a conscientious student in one of my writing classes, mentioned me in her paper, assessing the need for "multicultural" courses at the college where I teach. She observed that in our class discussions I often alluded to election year politics, and the typical response from her fellow writers was blankness in their weary eyes.

So I was inspired. I sat down at my home PC, and frantically pounded on the keyboard. Instead of the "laissez-faire" approach I had originally planned and promised my students for their third paper, and between reasoning, coaxing, and blackmailing, I *assigned* them another topic instead: "If I were to vote today. . . " This would still be their *own* paper, I promised. They were *free* to vote for anyone for any number of good reasons. Suspicious and reluctant, they pleaded "political illiteracy," but eventually bought it.

Of course, there were strings attached to the assignment: invention, revision, subject, audience, purpose, critical thinking, research, documentation, and all those buzz words—unity, coherence, emphasis, development, clarity and all those good old values.

What candidate won the heart of my students? Well, I didn't bother to count. All I know is that they certainly had some fun. Just look at the range of their choices, almost a duplicate of the Great Chain of Being: from the Almighty God to Mickey Mouse and Kermit the Frog all the way down to some notable specimens of *Homo sapiens:* Forrest Gump, Montel Williams, David Letterman, Rush Limbaugh, Clinton, Dole, Buchanan, H. Ross Perot, the list went on.

Is a candidate's character a relevant issue? Some of my students complained that too much time has been spent on who the president sleeps with, or why he does not sleep with his wife. "Who really cares about the president's sex life?" one of my students shrugged her shoulders. And I found myself nodding in agreement.

Paris had his Helen. Caesar had his Cleopatra. Empress Wu had her male courtiers. Mao had his Saturday night dances in the Forbidden City. JFK had his Marilyn (though it was only a one-night stand). The Prince of Wales had (and still has) his Camilla. And Princess Di had her...

How boring politics would be without love, romance, and adultery! At least, we'd have lost one of the greatest epics of all time, and one of the most uplifting fairy tales, or soap operas, if you prefer.

Bang! A student boxed my ears. "Anyone who's cheated on his wife would have no qualms about cheating on the whole nation, stupid!" Okay, okay, I admit that out of a weakness for drama, I'd *momentarily* relaxed in my moral vigilance.

Is the ability to fix the economy important? Certainly! Almost all the students were calling for a new president who'd be able to create new high-tech jobs, guarantee affordable college education and wipe out the ever-growing national debt. What's the number again? Two students reminded me in their collaborative paper that it is $5,071,791,748,467.89 as of March 30, 1996!

Frightened by its sheer monstrosity, I had to think creatively. Why don't we simply team up the First Lady, who has an excellent record in commodities trading, and the ex-presidential hopeful and red-flannel-shirted Lamar Alexander, who has an even more impressive record: $1 grew into $620,000.00 in a couple of years! So, let's do some simple arithmetic. With a 620,000% growth rate, all we need to kill the Goliath is $8,180,309.27. Steve Forbes and Ross Perot, with their deep pockets, surely wouldn't mind pitching in (hasn't Forbes spent around $28 million just to show he cares?). So, it would be painless for all of us. And it won't even take 7 years! No more taxes (progressive, or flat). No more trickle-down, or bottom-up economics. Just learn a few of the tricks, and play Wall Street.

I caught myself daydreaming.

Does the skin color or gender of a candidate matter? One of my students declared it's totally irrelevant whether the next

Election Year Blues on the Sideline

president is "black or white, or even pink with purple polkadots for all I care!" or where they are "male or female," or anything in between. But skin color and gender do seem to matter. Just listen to all the heated discussion about multiculturalism, ethnocentrism, immigration and affirmative action (didn't I overhear grumblings at my college about recent new hires of deeper hues weakening the faculty?). A few students went whole-heartedly for Buchanan's idea of erecting walls along the many miles of the U.S.-Mexican border. Others argued that it'd mean another Berlin Wall. Mexico would be walled out, but we'd all be walled in.

That's also why quite a number of students made their passionate pleas to Gen. Colin Powell to get into the race: he's yet to hear the calling in his soul, at least not yet in 1996.

Most of the time I was morally vigilant. Whenever a student tried to dismiss Dole as being too old, and too near his Maker (several of them said this), I would rise to the occasion and scribble indignantly in the margin: "Age discrimination, pal!"

It turned out that almost all the students had some fun working on this paper. I remember the fun I had back in 1992. Between writing my papers as a student, teaching Freshman composition, waiting on tables and delivering pizzas, I still found time to cheer on the sidelines during that year's election: from the primaries all the way to the inauguration.

One of the most entertaining moments was a debate between the three Vice Presidential candidates. I was so amused, watching the confused, tongue-tied, monosyllabic, and sometimes stuttering Gen. James Stockdale (a honorable, Vietnam War POW-turned-Perot running mate) caught in the crossfire between the ex-straight-A, scholar Gore, who is fluent but wooden, and the ex-straight-C scholar Quayle, who was relatively quick and effortless in speech.

As I glance at the place where I hail from in the rear-view mirror, I feel so sorry for the folks back there. Why do they have to twist arms and make deals behind closed doors in joyless, smoke-filled rooms, pulling long, somber faces, without the benefit of camcorders?! How much fun they're missing out there!

I've also tried to find time to cheer on the sidelines this year. But somehow, the excitement has dissipated. Too many issues to sort out. Too complicated, and too divisive. Too many promises which will be broken too easily. Too much demagoguery, and too mean-spirited.

Then, there is too much to do: juggling between a 15-credit-hour teaching load, piles of student papers, committee responsibilities, student advising, driving my son to his orthodontist and to his piano lessons, getting my 12-year-old Accord fixed, etc. Too much everything, and too little time to sit down and watch C-SPAN, to read the latest issue of *Time* and to follow the candidates as they baby-kiss along their campaign trails.

Now, I can appreciate why there was such a blankness in the weary eyes of my students. And I don't blame them if they choose to watch Letterman at the end of a long, exhausting day. He is, as one of my students asserted, "an intelligent man with a wit that can charm the pants off of you." "He would bring a bit of spice to the White House." At least, I might add, Letterman's "Top Ten List" seems more inspired than the ten-item list in the "Contract with America" signed unilaterally by the high-minded "Newtonic" Republicans.

I am grateful to Ms. Leona Baughman, and don't regret that I changed my assignment. Besides the fun they've had voting their hearts, my students have learned something about presidential politics. A democracy is a democracy is a democracy, despite all its flaws, and a democracy can't flourish with an illiterate (literally, or politically) populace and with less than a 50% voter turnout. I hope they'll all (95% of them are first-time voters) find the time to visit the polls coming November.

In the meantime, I'll remain a spectator. I can't wait to cross the line, and cast my own first vote. As an *independent* Independent.

Then what?

Olympic Fervor Felt First-hand in China

AUGUST 30, 1996

IT'S EVERYWHERE.

It's glaring in the papers' headlines, sparkling on the 24-hour live TV screens, dancing in the sound bites of radios, and radiating from the faces of brisk pedestrians, chatty cabbies, sweaty passengers in crowded buses and retirees playing the slow-motioned *tai chi* in the dewy parks. It's in the very air you breathe, and the hot midsummer sun doesn't seem to help relieve the fervor a bit.

The Centennial Olympic flames were burning gloriously at Atlanta, and I was to experience it all in China.

Forget about the tiresome daily routines. Forget about the floods pounding on the dams and banks of the Yangtze River. Forget about the soaring prices, and your sleepless envy of the next door neighbor who made a fortune overnight. The Olympic Games are on, and you have to seize the moment. You have to live it.

Days before the athletes were leaving Beijing for Atlanta, oath-taking rallies were staged. These rallies were graced by the presence of the nation's top leaders who called upon the young Olympians to do honor to the motherland, which they dutifully pledged to do, by bringing home more gold medals.

From the day the first gold medal was won by *judoka* Fuming Sun to the sixteenth by Guoliang Liu in Men's Single Table Tennis, the nation was caught in a roller-coaster ride, rising high with breathless joy, and plunging deep into abysmal disappointment. Every day, the China Central TV would replay all the award ceremonies featuring the five-starred red flag and the "March of the Brave Volunteers."

Written during the early days of the bloody WWII, when Japan began its aggressive venture in China, the melody of the Chinese national anthem strikes into the hearts of its listeners with a sense of life-and-death urgency, of crisis and glory, of epic and tragedy. It boils up in your arteries, gives you an adrenaline rush and makes you shiver with goose bumps, much as the "Star-Spangled Banner" does to its responsive American listeners. Or as the world famous, 60-proofChinese liquor, *Maotai*, did to such dignitaries as Henry Kissinger during one of his secret trips to Beijing in the early 1970's. The ritualistic replay would snowball as the medal count rose.

I went up to a shoe counter in a department store. My salesgirl was engaged in an excited recount with another salesgirl, manning a counter 15 feet away from hers. She was effusive over the story of Yifu Wang who had lost his sure gold medal in shooting due to a severe headache: "He fainted the second he let go the rifle." Spoiled as I was by receiving better service on the American side of the Pacific, I nevertheless listened to the already familiar story respectfully while waiting for the girl to put a semicolon, or at least a comma, in her narration.

As I was watching the U.S.-China women's soccer championship game, sitting in a couch near the window of my brother's first-floor apartment, I suddenly felt a shadow closing upon me from behind. Turning around, I confronted a pair of big eyes in a face pressed flat against the window-panes. A thirty-ish male passerby had joined us from outside, uninvited and unapologetic. And strange enough, I didn't even find that intrusive.

Don't tell me the Olympics is purely about friendship and testing human limits. Ever since the first game, held in the midsummer of 776 BC, at the Peloponnesian Peninsula, the Olympics has rarely been free of politics or nationalistic rivalry. Remember the Greek soldier named Phidippides who in 490 BC, ran the 26 miles from the Battle of Marathon to Athens? He died after screaming "Nike," the Greek are victorious over the Persians.

So the Chinese shouldn't have been upset at Bob Costas' begrudging comments when the Chinese delegation marched into the Olympic Stadium at the opening ceremony. Neither should they be angry that the United States government used all its superpower muscles to twist arms so that China's almost sure bid to hold the 2000 Olympic Games was foiled.

Neither should Rush Limbaugh have whined about the incumbent Clintons utilizing the Olympic torches to recharge their reelection campaign battery. Or had he conveniently forgotten what his hero Reagan did in his own time, in Los Angeles?

Olympic Fervor Felt First-Hand in China

Don't tell me that the motto of the Olympics is *Citius, Altius, Fortius*. When it comes down to it, it's all about the (gold) medal count. It's who's faster, higher, and stronger. Much as in the space race: it's not about humans conquering the space. Rather, it's about whether a Russian dog named Laika was the first to be launched into the space, or whether an American named Neil Armstrong was the first to walk on the moon.

So I wasn't surprised when the CCTV replayed, over and again, the footage of Dot Richardson's fly ball sailing, unmistakably, toward the foul pole in the gold-medal game. It being ruled fair regardless, the Chinese girls were shaken visibly, so were the millions of viewers back at home in China. I wanted to walk up to the sobbing girls on the TV screen, and pat them on the back, saying "It sucks, but hey. . . "

Neither was I annoyed by the loud homecoming parades given to the Olympians. After all, Michael Johnson's face twice commanded the cover of *Time*, and glittered I don't know how many times on NBC. But I did notice a hint of awkwardness in Yaping Deng, who claimed two gold medals in table tennis, and Xiaoshuang Li, the all-around gold medalist in men's gymnastics, when praises were being showered upon them as national heroes. They would have to endure such homecoming rituals many times more when they got back to their home provinces, cities, counties, townships, and of course, their own neighborhoods.

The final gold medal count (16 vs. 44) may signify how far behind China really is, not only in sports, but also in overall social and economic prowess. But behold, the winged Dragon of the Orient is hurrying near! As measured by the recently announced $33 billion trade deficit with China, and as forecast by the renowned futurist John Naisbitt in his *Megatrends Asia* (1996).

I don't know yet where I will be watching the Turn of the Millennium Olympic Games. I only hope it will prove to be a few inches closer to the Olympic ideal and its motto.

It's the Names, Stupid!

MARCH 4, 1997

"CALL ME ISHMAEL."
Thus begins the narrator in Herman Melville's voluminous novel, Moby Dick. Melville didn't bother to instruct his contemporary readers how to pronounce the name, knowing that they were mostly God-fearing Christians who were familiar with the story of that lonely wanderer (he did warn, though, that "h" in "whale" should not be left unsounded, "out of ignorance").

But pronouncing personal names properly has become quite a challenge.

When I began to learn English, many springs ago in a land where a very different tongue is spoken, I somehow got the impression that all English-speaking kids were called either John or Jane, and were from a family of either the Smiths or the Jones. Now, however, rosters for my college classes often read like a who's who of the ambassadors to the United Nations.

At the beginning of each semester, I labor over the rosters, rolling each name over in my mouth several times before venturing into the classroom. Experience has taught me that a slight deviation from correctness can inflict serious psychological injury on those who have zero tolerance for imperfection, at least when their names are at stake.

"C'mon, it's just a name," you might shrug your shoulders.

But a name is not just a matter of convenience that keeps one from confusing all the Johns with each other. It is who you are and where you are from. Indeed, it's a badge of cultural (religious, racial, linguistic, etc.) as well as personal identity. That's perhaps why *John* becomes *Sean, Giovanni, Johann, Hans, Jean, Jan, Ivan,* and *Yuehan* in other cultures, though all these can be traced back to the name of the person who baptized Jesus.

Of course, most Western names, first or last, except a

It's the Names, Stupid!

handful like Goldsmith, Shepherd, or Longfellow, have become opaque: the cultural and personal "meaning" is not translucent any more.

The meaning of many a non-Western name, however, is still readily accessible, if you happen to be from the same culture. A Chinese name, for example, can incorporate a dream, an inspiration, or a philosophy of life.

My wife's first name, *Xiaohong,* conjures up a breathtaking picture of the sun bursting upon the horizon at dawn. It was the view her father saw through the hospital window the morning she was born.

The first name of a friend of mine working at the same college, *Jiangchao,* born into an artists' family, evokes "a great river and torrential tides" and his last name, *Wang,* the majesty of a "king." Just say his full name aloud, and you get to know all there is to know about the sublime. Anyone who has seen his works, wherein is a delightful union of the Chinese and the Western painting traditions, can bear witness that he has lived up to his parents' great expectations.

The original Chinese name, *Da-i,* of *Time's* Man of the Year for 1996, David Ho, means the "Great One." This is a Daoist term, conceptualizing the cosmological vastness in a single essential element. No wonder this pioneer researcher cut through the diagnostic mess enmeshing the AIDS epidemic, and pinpointed the culprit for a panicking world: "It's a virus, stupid!"

Am I getting too mystical?

Back in 1990, thinking like a good Chinese, I spent many hours debating which English first name should I give my son. Finally, I settled on *Frank.* It didn't seem as opaque as most other names. Not too long ago, I was driving home and heard some pundit-journalist on NPR announcing his most recent discovery: the singing legend Frank Sinatra aside, few if not none of the rich and the famous today go by that first name anymore. So much for my investment in that name.

But again, a name is not just a name.

When everybody is on a first name basis, a professor and his/her students, a CEO and the janitor, a kid and his/her grandparents, or the President of the United States and the owner of a small restaurant in a place called Little Rock, you see democracy in action.

It's so much more liberating than a culture governed by the Confucian ideal of order and hierarchy. The *Shou* in my name, for example, is a given from a table designed by respected patriarchs in the Qi clan. Those who have a *Shou* in his/her name, 70 years old or born yesterday, are ensured of the same generational status. No room for trespassers.

Yet there is at least one redeeming virtue in the modern Chinese appellation custom: a woman gets to keep her own maiden name when married. An adoption of that alien practice could save many a woman here the pain of identity crisis when they, by choice or by necessity, have to march down the aisle more than once in their lifetime. It could be a source of confusion, though. When I went to a Christmas party at my wife's workplace back in Illinois, a name tag with her last name *Wang* on it was ready for me to pick up, I was Mr. *Wanged* the whole evening, and I had to play along good-humoredly.

But the real problem with a name other than Anglo-Saxon lies in its sound: staring at the spelling, you are clueless as to how to pronounce it without embarrassing all parties involved.

THAT'S WHY I WASN'T UPSET at all during the post-election days, when all the talk show hosts had so much fun, trying so hard to mispronounce *Huang, Trie,* and other names of the President's wealthy Asian friends and overzealous fundraisers.

Indeed, I have more than zero tolerance for people who mispronounce names. Last month, a rep from my dental insurance left a message on my answering machine about an unsolved problem. After introducing herself with professional ease, she began to trip and stumble: "This is a call for Mr. . . Oh, I really don't know how to say your name, *Quee? Quai?* I'm sorry if I pronounced it wrong. Is this Mr. . . *Q - I*, forgive me. . . ."

I could feel her level of embarrassment and frustration, and would have come to her rescue right there, "Relax, it's just a name!"

In one of my first classes at the college where I teach, I wanted to give the students some cues as to pronouncing my last name: "Just call me *Chi,*" I said, helpfully, "As a matter of fact, I own a couple of *Chi-Chi's* in town. Just mention my name to the hostess, and you'll automatically get a fifty percent discount."

One student sitting in the back of the room, whose attention had seemed to be drifting, straightened up his neck and asked, earnestly: "Which one?"

Yes, non-Anglo-Saxon names are quite a challenge to pronounce correctly. Little wonder (though it has baffled me for so long) whenever the word "diversity" is uttered, symptoms of trauma appear all over the faces of tender-hearted folks. "It's the names, stupid!"

Tiger! Tiger!

JANUARY 7, 1998

AS THE CHINESE YEAR OF THE TIGER was drawing near, I decided to venture into the cyber-forest: to search for that mystical fire that had so inspired the visionary English poet, William Blake (1757–1827). I'm happy to report to the world that, in that jungle of wild life, the fire in the eyes of the deified feline is burning as bright as ever.

Browsing via *Yahoo!* for tigers, I scored 506 sightings, and via *Lycos* I got 10,390 hits. In the cyber-jungle, tigers of all species roam freely. But the Tiger seems to be most prosperous in the field of sports. Numerous athletic teams, pro or amateur, love to invoke the ferocious feline as their source of inspiration: For handball, you have Gothenburg Tigers; for soccer, Dayton Tigers; for baseball, Detroit Tigers; for skydiving, Flying Tigers; for softball, Northport Tigers; for rugby, Balmain Tigers; for swimming, Missouri Tigers; and for basketball, Mansfield Lady Tigers.

In this misty midst are more than a dozen Tiger Woods Shrines set up for the convenience of his worshipful fans, so that they don't need to stir one step from their own habitats for a pilgrimage.

Quite a number of websites, however, are devoted to the preservation of the real Tiger. Of these, the most impressive is Tiger Watch by a 13-year-old called Mez Hopking. According to Mez, worldwide, tigers have all but vanished, and may now number as few as 5,000. Of the world's remaining five subspecies, three are close to extinction: there are only an estimated 30 to 80 South China Tigers, 150 to 200 Siberian Tigers and 600 to 650 Sumatran Tigers left in the wild.

So, the fire for the Tiger is not burning as bright in the real forests.

The reason is simple: Humans have always had a love-hate relationship with the Tiger. According to Simon Barnes, a well-known wildlife and conservation writer, in the days when tigers were more ubiquitous, people who lived in or near the forests of Asia had to come to terms with the Tiger, the most fierce and uncompromising animal.

The essential thing was how to cope with life alongside tigers who would boldly wander into villages at any time. For people before the days of firearms, the ferocity of the Tiger was not a myth, but an everyday fact. How many human lives has the Tiger claimed? One estimate puts the number in the past 400 years somewhere around one million; that's about 2,500 a year.

Yet the Tiger has always fascinated humans. It, in fact, has always been an important part of Chinese as well as other Asian mythologies. For the Chinese, the Tiger is the king of the beasts and the lord of land animals. The Chinese god of wealth used to ride a tiger. In old Asian animist belief systems, you should not be so disrespectful as to refer to the Tiger by name directly. Instead, one should call the big cat "the hairy-face," or "the striped one."

The Tiger is also one of the twelve beasts of the Chinese zodiac. A person born in the Year of the Tiger is said to be born lucky. Tiger people, according to some, are risk-takers by nature. They are sensual, enthusiastic, impulsive and can be hell to live with. If you happen to pick up one of those placemats in a Chinese restaurant, you will find that the Tiger is forthright, sensitive, courageous and most compatible with the horse (born in 1990, 1978, etc.) and the dog (born in 1994, 1982, etc.), yet antagonistic to the monkey (in born 1992, 1980, etc.).

For all these honors, however, the Tiger has paid dearly.

The Chinese and their Asian neighbors—Koreans, Japanese, Thai and other East Asians—believe in the medicinal miracles associated with the Tiger: a belief and practice that goes back more than 1,000 years. To them, nearly every part of a tiger has some medicinal benefit: the eyeballs are used to treat epilepsy; the tail for various skin diseases; the bile for convulsions in children; whiskers for toothaches; and the brain for laziness. The bones, however, are the most valued. They can be ground into powder before being made into pills, or cut into segments and soaked in wine. Drinking ten ml of tiger

Tiger! Tiger!

wine twice daily is said to relieve "wind" ailments such as headaches and "cold" ailments such as rheumatism.

It is not clear, though, whether the fixation has anything to do the tiger's sexual prowess. According to zoologists, once a pair of tigers embark on serious courtship, it rapidly becomes a honeymoon of epic proportions. They can be at it for days on end. While strict counting is impossible for wild tigers, statistics of performance in zoos are awesome: one observation puts the figure at 106 copulations in four days, another at 52 times in a single day; intervals in between can be as short as five minutes. The gold medal, regrettably, goes to the Lion whose record is 157 times in 55 hours.

The shrinking tiger population can be attributed to many major factors. War, modern agriculture, pest control, habitat loss and trophy hunting have all played their part. Prince Philip, accompanied by her Majesty Queen Elizabeth II, contributed by killing two tigers in 1961, on one of their tours of India.

Having learned from its past mistakes, China, along with other Asian countries, has made some valiant efforts to protect whatever is left of its tiger population. China passed the Wild Animal Protection Law in 1988, and its Ministry of Forestry lists 21 reserves within the presumed range of the Tiger.

Between love and hate, humans have made it more than difficult for the Tiger and other animals to survive. It is high time we quit our "barbaric" sport of pigeon shooting, fox hunting and tiger poaching. Will we one day have to resort to cloning as the final savior of all the endangered species?

As the Year of the Tiger (or the Hairy-face, or the Striped One, to be more respectful) approaches, I wish the world peace and prosperity, and may the fire for the famed feline burn as bright as in Blake's time!

What's Up?

Presidential Sex Scandals, The Law of the Smelly Bean Curd, and Other Trivia

MARCH 9, 1999

OK, LET ME ADMIT up front: I was a Clinton-sex-scandal-Interngate-Clintongate-Sexgate-whatever-name-you-call-it junkie. I was hooked to it. I experienced a real high from every latest development. All right, I'm being a bit hyperbolic, but the truth of the matter is I was interested. More interested than I know I should have been, and more so than most people would like to admit.

Back in 1996, I had a mild case of election-year blues, as I mentioned in a previous essay, written during that year. Bored by excessive demagoguery that was being drummed up by vote-chasing candidates, and utterly exhausted by too many personal and professional responsibilities, I did not have the energy to follow the Oval Office aspirants on their campaign trails, and watch them kiss babies at rallies. I yawned every time Kenneth Starr and his hired bloodhounds sniffed up suspiciously, but not incriminatingly, dirty linen or footprints from the Whitewater scandal, and all of its fledgling scandals: Filegate, Travelgate, you name it.

From January 21, 1998, however, things began to take a dramatic turn. When the new round of scandals—sex scandals, mind you—was first made public, I knew that presidential politics had just taken on new life. All it took was the footage of a young and handsome president (a 50-ish president should be considered quite youthful), hugging a twentysomething, young and sexy (at least the way she swings her body, cocks her head and locks in the whole person of the President knowingly with her sparkling big bold eyes) ex-intern. When some good folks thought Monica Lewinsky's story was "so tawdry, and so devastating" that she might have made it all up, I had the good sense and foresight to buy it right

—163—

away. It was so energizing. Finally, there was something worth watching!

I, unapologetically, subscribe to the truth, universally unacknowledged, that all men and women in possession of normal desires are in want of sex scandals (not necessarily courting sex scandals themselves, but consuming juicy news of sex scandals committed by others).

All right, the epithet "all" may be an overgeneralization. Let me rephrase it by quoting, at the risk of being narcissistic, from my earlier essay on election-year blues: politics would be so boring without love, romance and sex scandals. Indeed, many people have professed their disgust, their disdain and eventually their boredom with it all. I believe that these morally upright folks are genuinely disgusted, and have been telling the truth, the whole truth, and nothing but the truth, in protesting how they feel in the bottom of their hearts.

But, like it or not, sex scandals involving the President—JFK, LBJ, FDR, or Thomas Jefferson, for that matter, who is now known through the magic of DNA testing to have engaged in extramarital affairs—always acquire a charm and beauty of epic dimensions. They always prove irresistible and capable of penetrating any Maginot Line (or TMD—Theater Missile Defense system the United States has been talking about building recently) of moral defense you could build around yourself. And I have very little doubt that among folks who have solemnly professed their disgust or disdain or boredom, there are a few who have thus professed just to show their moral superiority—imagined or real—not only to the President, but also to those who are openly addicted to scandals.

It reminds me of a Chinese delicacy that used to be very popular. It is a kind of preserved bean curd that has an uninviting dark bluish color, and a very strong and repugnant smell. In fact, the smell is so repugnant that one whiff of it on a hot summer day would knock you right out. Yet this unsightly and smelly delicacy redeems itself in the eating because it tickles the taste buds in a strange and wonderful and indescribable way. I tried it—with all its dripping, sticky sauce—a few times when I was a young boy, and never developed a liking for it. Even today, I still do not know what nutritional value or medicinal benefits it offers besides its pungent taste, but many Chinese folks simply love it, and do not mind the repulsive smell at all.

At any rate, The Law of the Smelly Bean Curd—allow me to be the discoverer of a new law, at least once in my lifetime—

clearly applies to Clinton's sex scandals. It explains why, while so many people have loudly complained about being sick of it all, the show keeps airing new episodes and even more incredible admissions. And there is no sign of when the final curtain will fall. The reason is simple: it attracts a huge audience whose appetite for drama or melodrama is almost insatiable.

I know, I know, there is another law that governs the universe, too: the Law of Diminishing Returns. Too large a dose of any scandal—even presidential sex scandals—for too long will eventually induce boredom. Period. There is one noticeable difference, though: those who like the smelly bean curd do not need to be equivocal or apologetic about it, while few people would like to admit openly that they are presidential sex scandal junkies. It involves a certain degree of hypocrisy which, being harmless, shall be left alone here.

Besides an innate craving for drama, my addiction can be explained by a somewhat nobler curiosity of mine. Being a Chinese, I came to the States too late to experience Nixon's Watergate firsthand. When the five Nixon boys broke into and wiretapped the Democratic Party's headquarters on the evening of June 17, 1972, I was a 10th grader, living in a far away country still caught in the turmoil of the last years of the Cultural Revolution.

I count myself as the kind of person who believes that there is a world of difference between reading about a historical event years after it happened, and living through history firsthand while it is still being made. I have to confess, though I hate to do so, that I did feel somewhat fortunate that I was at the right time, and at the right place, when the Clinton-Monica saga burst on the airwaves and landed on the front pages. I could watch it as it was, and is, still unfolding. I wanted to find out more about this exciting and mystifying place called "The United States of America."

In case anyone still has lingering doubts about the universally unacknowledged truth or the Law of the Smelly Bean Curd promulgated above, just look at the headlines major television networks employed in covering the Clinton sex scandal on Day One: ABC: Crisis in the White House; CNN: Investigating the President; Fox News: Sex Scandal; NBC: Investigating the President; CBS: White House Under Fire. Listen to their solemn drum-beating, their blood-stirring background music. One would think that the country was in the throes of a crisis of the same magnitude as Pearl Harbor on the morning of December 7, 1941.

Time, not losing a beat, though not as fast as its television cousins, followed quickly with its own sensational headline on its February 2, 1998 special report: "Monica and Bill: The Sordid Tale That Imperils the President." The cover featured a picture of a victorious Clinton (who had just won the reelection), and a coquettish Monica (who had been waiting, brokenhearted, for him to pick up the phone, and call her back to services in the White House) sharing a fleeting moment of intimacy together in public. This notorious picture was printed and paraded a million times again, and has since sneaked its way into the deep recesses of millions of peoples' memories worldwide.

During the yearlong ordeal—a more accurate word for the whole mess—which officially ended on February 12, 1999, when the Senate delivered its "not guilty" verdict, *Time* had Clinton on its cover no less that 15 times. Its pursuit of the scandal culminated in electing Clinton, Man of the Year 1998, a dubious distinction he was to share with his tormentor, Kenneth Starr.

Mainstream media such as *Time*, CBS, NBC and ABC, have always prided themselves on their moral seriousness and superiority, and are never hesitant to show their disdain for tabloids like the *Globe*, the *Star*, Inside Edition and Hardy Copy. In many ways, they have earned their pride, but in relentlessly chasing after the Clinton scandal as well as other sensational news stories, OJ, JonBenet Ramsey, Princess Di, to name just a few, they have proven to be birds of the same feather. They have been just as unscrupulous, leaving no "salacious detail" unexplored and unexploited.

Being very thoughtful and viewer/reader friendly, they even provide visual aids, e.g., the floor plan of the White House—the "crime scene" which includes the Oval Office, the study, and the hallway—lest their readers and viewers would not be able to visualize where Monica and her very "sensual" and "tender" soulmate were being intimate. The only difference between mainstream media and comedians like Jay Leno and David Letterman is that comedians profit from the scandal by making people roar with laughter, while mainstream media have to do it with a straight face.

What about the average Joe and Jane on Main Street, America? Do they love the story? You bet! They can't get enough of it. According to watchers of the media, the saga virtually held dominion everywhere during the first week of its life, from radio to television to morning papers and magazines.

If the ratings did not go up and papers did not sell, do you think the media would not quickly fall out of love by directing their gallantry elsewhere?

Even on the Web, it was the sex scandal all the time. *Time's* website hit rate doubled, and the website of every other major media experienced a similar jump. The *New York Times* on the Web hit 2.5 million visitors per day during the first week. That figure easily beat the 1 million record, set right after the death of Princess of the Wales September, 1997.

Even weeks after everybody thought it was officially over, when people from left and right, up and down, had protested for the thousandth time that they had had more than enough, more than they cared to know, millions—72 million, to be exact—flocked to ABC's "20/20" on the evening of March 3, 1999.

For what? Just to have another dose of the scandal, to watch and hear the notorious ex-intern pour out her mixed feelings for the "Big Creep," passing her unflattering judgments on Linda Tripp and Kenneth Starr, and sharing her pain with the rest of the nation. OK, "pain" was probably not an accurate word here because she seemed to be having such a good time reliving the past by talking about it to the world.

Indeed, one could not help but get the impression that this must be the moment of her life she had been dreaming of. She seemed to be savoring every second of it. Of course, ABC decided to run this Barbara Walters exclusive interview not out of any humanitarian concern for the psychological well being of its faithful viewers. What it was fishing for was the ratings and it was not to be disappointed with a hefty 47% of the market share.

Even the Chinese media have been following the ups and downs of the Clinton saga. Of course, because of their belief in modesty and moderation, they would not use any eye-catching headlines, or indulge in "salacious" details. Still, the impact of the Clinton sex scandal was unmistakably felt. No less than the *People's Daily*, mouthpiece of the Party (CCP), covered the sex scandal and the impeachment trial regularly—usually on page 5 or 6, devoted to world news—to keep its readers abreast of what was going on. Its web edition has a special feature giving a detailed chronology of the scandal, too. CCTV (China Central Television) also found a place for the scandal in its 15-minute and 30-minute news programs whenever there was a new turn.

Why? I believe there was a genuine concern about whether Clinton would be able to survive the scandal, and how it would impact U.S.-China relations. It took years for the fragile relations to stabilize again. This did not happen until the beginning of Clinton's second term. But beyond that justification, the Law of the Smelly Bean Curd is in full effect there, too.

Sensational news such as sex scandals involving a president as handsome and youthful as Bill Clinton, who had visited China not too long before, would certainly help sell newspapers and other publications. Take the *People's Daily* again.

Since the introduction of market factors into media services, its subscription rate has been falling steadily from 6 million to about 3 million, according to a recent panel discussion on CCTV. It now has to compete with hundreds, if not thousands, of other publications that do not have to tote the Party line as much, and are run by more savvy editors. It has to delicately balance what is newsworthy, and what readers like to read. I doubt, though, that reporting the Clinton sex scandal would have in any way boosted its subscription numbers since other newspapers and publications had been exploiting the unfolding sex scandal, too, only far more boldly.

Youth Reference, a supplement of *China Youth Daily*, a major Chinese newspaper whose targeted readers are the young and educated—particularly college students and graduates—even carried a piece on the alleged affair between Susan McDougal and Clinton. Based on a story from the tabloid, *Star*, and rewritten in Chinese by a Chinese expatriate in the United States, it portrayed the alleged affair as a touching love story in which a heroine would rather languish in jail, than betray her paramour of a bygone time.

If presidential sex scandals are always sensational and tantalizing, this one was particularly so. It had all the necessary ingredients to cook up something really soapy. Hear me out.

THE TWISTED PLOT: suspenseful, full of surprising turns and unexpected reversal of fortunes, the denouement tantalizingly beyond prediction, spiced up by power, love, hate, and sex—kinky sex, for that matter—, intrigue, a "right-wing conspiracy" and an even more cynical counter-conspiracy theory (Bill and Hilary have been ghostwriting the scripts of the saga just to improve their ratings).

Flawed Characters: much despised, Ahab-like heroes and slippery yet lovable villains, star-struck young temptresses and 50-ish hormone-driven victims, loyal servants and treacherous friends, walk-on characters like Saddam Hussein who came to

Clinton's rescue at every critical juncture in his political life by taunting the U.S.

Spectacle: who can rival the major networks with their high-tech presentations and talent pool in this category?

And, of course, there was the standing room only audience, always craving more.

I AM NOT SURE if there is truth to the claim that a nation gets the leaders it deserves. Neither do I know how to take the *Time*/CNN poll, conducted in early February, 1998 that showed 54% of Americans think Clinton's moral standards are "about the same as the average married man's." However, a little scene I witnessed inadvertently in the waiting room of a local car dealership should be somewhat telling.

It was close to the end of December, 1998, when the to-impeach-or-not-to-impeach quarrel was reaching a throat-cutting madness in the House. I was waiting for my Mazda Protégé. It was being serviced for a nagging noise that came from somewhere under the hood.

As usual, I picked up a copy of *USA Today*, turned its pages aimlessly to help cope with the awkwardness of finding myself among a group of strangers in a crammed space. In the waiting room, there were three or four other customers, each busy with something that would divert attention away from the mind-numbing wait one has to put up with under such circumstances. Hanging high in the corner was a 20-inch color TV on which CNN anchors were talking excitedly about the latest development in you-know-what.

A black woman, in her late 30s, who could not hold it to herself anymore, was the first to break the code of silence among the strangers. In a rather angry voice, she warned that the Republicans had better leave the man alone because what had happened should be the kept between the man and his wife. It was no body else's business!

Her statement was seconded enthusiastically by a 60-ish white woman, who stood up and declared to the gathering in the room: "I have been married to my husband for over 40 years, and I know what men are like! As long as he's a good president, I can't care what he does in his personal life!"

But the real bombshell, to me at least, came from a man in his fifties, whose ethnicity I could not establish for sure (I'm supposed to be color blind, anyway): "I am sorry, but what 50-year-old man doesn't want to do it to a 20-year-old woman?!"

That does it! That's the most honest and truthful thing that I had heard anyone say during this whole saga. That holds the key to many—if not all—of the puzzles which have perplexed many a good, and morally upright American. You can explain Clinton's overwhelmingly high approval rate, despite the scandals, in terms of: 1) a great economy—the skyrocketing Dow Jones, low unemployment, low inflation, 2) the death of moral outrage—if you happen to believe Bill Bennet, 3) the disappearance of the Moral Majority—if you believe there has ever been such a majority in this country, 4) Clinton's good luck—of which he certainly has plenty, or 5) Clinton being a naughty but resilient comeback kid.

Americans' have a generous love for the underdog, the prodigal son. They also respect the borderline between one's public and private life (though this last one is somewhat dubious, judging by the zealous appetite people have shown for scandals). All these explanations may be true, though not completely satisfactory.

That man in his fifties may have put his finger right on it: Clinton has done something all men dream of doing. Most never dare to follow the dream to its fruition. According to scientists who study the phenomenon of love, men are in a perennial search for younger and physically more attractive, hence more fertile, women to make sure that their genes will spread far and wide, while women search for socially and financially more successful men to provide a secure home to nurture their young, hence the proverbial Seven Year Itch.

In the words of an anthropologist pundit, politics has often been "little more than reproductive competition:" men using power to better spread their genes, which accounts for the fact that emperors and kings used to have so many wives and concubines. There is a Chinese phrase that gives a numerical description of such imperial or royal indulgences: *san gong liu yuang*, meaning three palaces and six compounds, each packed with the prettiest, young girls selected (often with force) from all over the country.

Each of these young girls was expected to wait in her quarters for His Majesty to bestow his favor upon her some night. Many would languish, like caged birds, until their youth and beauty faded, never even having looked at the person of His Majesty.

Clinton's political aspirations may not be inspired by his restless genes, but didn't he confess to Monica, in a soul-shar-

What's Up? The Law of the Smelly Bean Curd ... 171

ing moment between them, that he had had more than 100 partners before he was 40?

Make no mistake that Clinton is not the lone victim of his own genes. Numerous, powerful men in today's political life have been led astray, and have committed "youthful indiscretions." The names that come to mind readily are Ted Kennedy, Bob Packwood, Henry Hyde, Newt Gingrich, Bob Livingston, as well as JFK, LBJ, FDR and the other presidential figures mentioned earlier.

These are the people who have the guts and power to follow their instincts. The rest of the crowd, who either have not acquired the necessary power or are fearful of consequences, go to the cinema.

They watch *Fatal Attraction*, the *English Patient*, the *Bridges of Madison County*, the *Titanic*, or *Shakespeare in Love*. There, they can identify with the heroes or heroines for two hours, to live their lives to the fullest, fulfill their wildest dreams. Then, they can return to face their mundane, everyday realities.

People read Stephen King and watch horror movies on the night of Halloween for pretty much the same reasons: to experience the scariest fear with safety, and to play out the darkest instincts deep in their conscious or unconscious, without actually being victimized by these instincts.

These average, normal folks would have exercised far more caution if they ever dared to follow their instincts. In fact, prudent lawyers and businessmen nowadays do not meet their clients or colleagues of the opposite sex in hotel rooms—a favorite place of Clinton's to meet young, female campaign staff. Even male college professors, just to be cautious, seem to be leaving their office doors open, or at least ajar, when holding one-on-one conferences with female students.

Some people have complained that if Clinton had exercised the slightest bit of restraint, complying with the minimal standards of presidential marital conduct, knowing that people like Kenneth Starr were hovering over him with a big net, he would not have had sex with a young intern in the White House. That is a big if, and that if is beside the point.

The truth of the matter is, if he hadn't done what he did, he would not be Clinton. Call it sheer stupidity, arrogance, moral depravity or sexaholism if you like, when power and powerful hormones join forces, there is no predicting what one will do—in spite of one's intelligence and full awareness of the potential consequences.

What about folks who have expressed their outrage at Clinton? It would be unfair to downplay their sense of morality, but isn't there a sense of jealousy, or sour grapes involved here? Deep down in our hearts, there is a mixture of love and hate, admiration and jealousy, for this guy. He seems to have gotten it all, and gotten away with it. We should not forget, though, that he has paid a heavy price, if we can take all of his public repentance for its face value. Those folks who hold a grudge against him, whether for personal or for political reasons, should at least draw some satisfaction in the deep humiliations he has suffered, and call it even.

Folks should lighten up and look at the silver lining around the dark cloud that has been hanging over the nation's sky. Come to think of it, the nation actually owes a lot to both Bill and Monica. The most obvious reason is for the entertainment they have provided. If you have listened to Jay Leno or David Lettermen, or watched any episode of "Saturday Night Live", you know what I mean. Such entertainment was particularly valuable when the nation was almost traumatized during the post-Seinfeld days when our multi-millionaire basketball players decided to go on strike.

The scandal has given folks, even young kids, once-in-a-lifetime opportunities to learn about things they should have learned in school. Without the scandal, such heavy topics as constitutional politics and impeachment would have bored people to death. Now, however, solemn-sounding legal terms like high crime, misdemeanor, obstruction of justice, abuse of power, tampering with witnesses, etc., have found their way into everyday parlance. Those who have benefited the most, of course, are aspiring, young lawyers and politicians who have had a fast-forward, futuristic vision of themselves leaving permanent marks on history.

Let me ask, how many high school kids had heard of names like Andrew Johnson and Richard Nixon before the impeachment process kicked off?

Linguistically, the scandal helped heighten young school children's sensitivity to the power of words. Before this, who could have imagined that simple words such as "is," "sex," and "alone" could be deconstructed, and interpreted in so many interesting ways?

Not the least among the beneficiaries of the scandal is the economy. It may sound cynical even to suggest it, but the scandal may have pumped millions—if not billions—of dollars into the economy, judging by the almost 50 million dollars that have been disposed of by Kenneth Starr in hunting down the President, the estimated 9 million dollars the Clintons owe their attorneys, the horrendous amount of gratuities the networks must have paid their special legal consultants, and the millions of dollars these networks have earned by selling commercials. Didn't ABC charge $800,000 for 30-second commercials on the "20/20" show in which Barbara Walters interviewed Monica exclusively? That is five times the normal ad rate.

Not to mention the many books that have been published, and will be published on the saga. By the way, if you want to purchase Monica's Story, from the hot online bookstore Amazon.com, you will pay $14.97, plus shipping and handling, instead of the list price $24.95. Go figure.

The last time I checked (March 7, 1999), it was ranked No. 1 in sales at Amazon. Even the producers of *Primary Colors* and *Wag the Dog* were hoping to jump on the scandal bandwagon to positively impact their box office receipts. I don't know if I would have gone to these two movies had it not been for what was going on in the other show business world of Washington, DC.

The scandal has even had a positive impact on the coming of age of the information superhighway. Some media pundits mused that the Clinton sex scandal has done for the Internet what FDR's fireside talks did for radio, and Kennedy's assassination did for TV.

The statistics mentioned earlier of the hits websites of major media experienced during the first week of the scandal offer convincing testimony to this speculation. The Internet certainly made it possible for the "salacious details" of Starr's report, and other documents to reach every accessible household in the world instantaneously, and made it available 24 hours a day for people to chew at any time they had a fancy to. At least, the first shot was first heard on the net. Which other media could rival that?

For folks who are still not consoled by all the positive things that have come out of the scandal, you should at least look at the whole deal from a historical perspective. When Paris abducted Helen, it must have been quite a catastrophic scandal then, judging by the voyages that were launched, the wars that were fought, the ships that were wrecked, and number of warriors and innocent women and children who perished. But the scandal gave birth to two of the greatest epics in the world of literature: the *Iliad* and the *Odyssey*.

When Caesar and Antony, each in turn, fell in love with

Cleopatra, it must have been quite a scandal for the high-minded Romans, too. See what Shakespeare and other great poets (John Dryden, for one) have done with it? Now we can enjoy masterpieces such as *Antony and Cleopatra* and *All for Love*.

Emperor Tang Xuanzong's love for his favorite concubine Yang—famed to be one of four, greatest babes in China's five thousand years of history—nearly cost him his throne. Then, what? A Peking opera classic called *The Tipsy Imperial Concubine (Gui Fei Cui Jiu)*, based upon this scandalous love story, has attracted big crowds of opera fans to the theaters for generations.

Who knows, someday someone with the literary genius comparable to that of Homer or Shakespeare may come along and create something equally impressive about Bill and Monica. You just have to be optimistic and exercise some patience.

In all seriousness, as far as I see it, the United States of America has stood the test, intact, and the State of the Union is strong. I do not know how many societies in the world today could have pulled through such a scandal—which has drawn all three branches of the government deep into the mess—without being at least partially paralyzed. Life on Main Street, America as well as on the Wall Street, has been going on without as much as a glitch.

In a way, the Beltway is almost irrelevant to the everyday life of the rest of the country, which speaks volumes for the strength and resiliency of this great nation. In addition, the whole thing, however disgusting and boring it is, is a healthy self-correcting process. The nation caught a cold, sneezed a bit, recovered quickly, and things moved on.

Yes, America is a land of numerous paradoxes, a mixture of the best and the worst, just as every other country in the world is. So cheer up. At least, not all presidents are victims of raging hormones. The worst sin Jimmy Carter has ever committed, according to his confession to the *Playboy* magazine during an interview, is to having lusted in heart. Who hasn't? There must be something wrong with a man if he has never committed adultery in such an innocent, harmless manner. The mark of a good man—really good man—is not whether he is free from such lustful instincts, but whether he can rein them in, and is still able to thrive.

Besides, there are moral policemen and policewomen patrolling everywhere. Dr. Laura's own past may not be stainless, but her moral crusade has certainly served the country well, even though sometimes she seems to come down on the morally confused callers too hard.

I sometimes wonder, though, what would have happened if Monica—in her most repressed days after Bill had dumped her—called Dr. Laura, instead of talking to a friend who would be taping the whole thing for the special prosecutor and the whole world to hear later. Would the United States and the world have been spared it all?

Well, it's no use speculating all that, now. Just one thought, though: could we end up with Dr. Monica on the airwaves one day? Just the thought of it. . .

At least you should be encouraged by one positive sign. On the night Barbara Walters' exclusive interview with Monica was aired, I—of all people—dozed off in the middle of it. When I woke up, Monica was already in the middle of sharing her suicidal thoughts with the anchor, and the rest of the world. Instead of regretting what I had missed, I reached for the remote and turned it off.

Enough is enough. I am glad that I've still got some moral dignity. I trust that I was not the only one among the 72 million people who tuned in that night and had the good sense to turn it off before it was over.

Life will go on. Even in the post-Monica era.

P.S.: When I picked up this week's issue of *Time*—March 11, 1999—in my mailbox, and looked at the cover, I knew right away how far off I had been in prematurely announcing the curtain fall for the whole show. Any man who has glanced at the cover but has not somehow been tickled by the innocent and guileless beauty in the repackaged face of the most famous ex-intern in the world should have ample reason to suspect that there is something amiss with his masculinity. Oh, America's love affair with Monica—and Clinton's sex scandal—is far from being over yet.

Forever Behind: Confessions of a Half-Hearted Hardy Fan

MAY, 1995

THE EVENING OF SEPTEMBER 23, 1994. JFK International Airport. After six years of having not seen me, and more than 15 hours of transpacific and transcontinental flight, across a dozen time zones, my parents finally walked towards me. Hug. Laugh. Tears. And a big lump in the throat. There was so much to celebrate and so much catching up to do. Yet the first thing my father did, with the shaking hands of a 65-year-old who had barely survived the blizzard of the Cultural Revolution, was to dig out of his carry-on bag a book. He thrust it into my hand. It was a copy of Thomas Hardy's *A Pair of Blue Eyes*. I had co-translated it eight years before.

It was one of those rare moments in one's life when the thing, long-expected and way overdue, has finally arrived. During the years after the completion of the translation, I had been like a young father, who has had everything to do with the creation of a new life, and yet at the time of birth has to wait outside the delivery room. To be shut out of the last stage of such a process is agony. In this case, the waiting happened to have been prolonged, the anxiety had been mounting, and there was little else anyone could do to help.

Indeed, the delayed arrival of this book symbolized the rather awkward position of a young scholar. During my 10-year long relationship with Hardy, I seemed to be falling forever behind and not able to catch on with whatever was the trend. This was the case when I was working on my master's thesis, and translating Hardy in the China of the 1980s where the old literary ideology, though challenged, still dominated. I was to find myself in a more awkward position at graduate seminars in the U. S. of the 90s where interpretative communities were singing a completely different tune.

Although it was very late when we finally got back to our home in Harrisburg, Pennsylvania, I locked myself in my little study to have an intimate moment alone with my book. Caressing the beautifully designed cover pages. Fondling every single word, font, color and pattern. Feverishly flipping through the pages to revisit the scenes that had challenged me the most and caused me so many a sleepless night due to their linguistic and cultural idiosyncrasies. These scenes proved to be the most delightful when they were finally captured with as little loss of beauty as possible in Chinese.

I signed the contract to translate *A Pair of Blue Eyes* near the end of 1985, when China was still caught in the tide of a revival of leaning which had begun fervently in the early 1980s. This was after years of cultural proletarianization. Classics from Western as well as Chinese literature were hot items in bookstores. Cervantes, Dante, Boccaccio, Chaucer and Shakespeare, translated by an older generation of scholars of foreign literature, were being revised and re-published. So were Hardy's major novels like *Tess of the d'Urbervilles*.

Riding the crest of this tidal wave, the editors at a prestigious publishing house, specializing in translations of foreign literature, were interested in undertaking a new project in Western Classics. Having finished my master's thesis on Hardy, I suggested *A Pair of Blue Eyes*. They liked it, and my partner, who was living in a different city, and I plunged into it with fervor.

I was responsible for translating the preface and Chapters 20–40, and with writing the translators' note. Both full-time college teachers, we had to burn a lot of midnight oil. To live up to the three cardinal principles of translation upheld in China—faithfulness, expressiveness and elegance—we often labored long over a particular word, phrase, or sentence to catch the spirit and color of the original, and recreate it in a very different target language.

To ensure stylistic consistency, we kept the post offices busy for quite some time by sending the manuscript of every chapter to each other for comments and revisions, creating a little tale of two cities of our own. At the busiest time, my wife, my father and my mother-in-law were mobilized to help "climb the squares," a Chinese expression for the slow process of copying manuscripts.

By the time the translation was done, it was almost 1987. By then, however, the renaissance seemed to have cooled off. With the economy switching to a market gear, the nation was caught in another fever. More and more people fell head over heels in a hot pursuit of dollar signs. Fewer and fewer people had the patience to chase the stars, or listen to the nightingale on the balcony. The pace of life was getting faster, and pop culture was the thing of the day.

Naturally, our publisher had difficulty promoting the sale, the orders from bookstores fell measurably short of the six thousand copies minimally required to break even. Thus, the proof of the book had been locked in the dark limbo of a storage room ever since, despite our repeated efforts with the editors.

Finally, early 1994, finding the waiting too suspenseful to our liking, and worried that a longer night of sleep for the book might bring even more and worse nightmares, we each offered to contribute 1000 *Yuan*, the equivalent of two months salary for a college professor, to resurrect the book. We could not afford to wait for another major revival of learning.

MY INFATUATION WITH HARDY began back in 1983 when I was searching for a topic for my master's thesis. It is one of those moments in one's life when we seem to know exactly what we want to do, and meanwhile are fretful, uncertain and overwrought with anxiety. It was then that I stumbled upon *Tess of the d'Urbervilles*. I came. I saw. And I was conquered.

I fell in love. It was a love mingled with an abundance of pity and fear. Then I checked out another of Hardy's novels. Another. Still another. Then, I made up my mind. I proposed the thesis, and was approved.

Hardy, of course, seemed a natural fit for a Marxist approach. As John Goode explains, a Marxist approach to the study of Hardy would be both historically and theoretically relevant though not without its problems. A Marxist approach to Hardy in the context of China would seem even more "relevant" for, as is well known, a simplistic or dogmatic Marxist approach had dominated the literary discourse there for quite some time. The landscape of Western literature, classic or modern, had been littered with footprints left by the specter of sinicized, Marxist criticism. A poor peasant girl goes to claim kin, and is victimized by an aristocratic rake? Nothing fits more conveniently than a reading through the lens of class struggle and materialistic determinism, which is exactly what is done in the translator's note for *Tess*. There is a lot of validity in such a reading. But I was not content.

There was another possible reading of Hardy that also had claims to relevancy in the context of Chinese society: sexual politics. Women in China, according to Mao Zedong, were exploited and repressed not only politically, economically and religiously, but also sexually.

At the bottom of the social structure based upon Confucian ideals, a girl had to obey her father, a wife had to obey her husband, and when she became a widow, she had to obey the son. Indeed, the double standard in sexual politics has operated on two planes. The rich and powerful—gentry classes, feudal lords and emperors from the great Tan and Han dynasties to Mao himself, as documented by his physician Li Zhisui in his 682-page *The Private Life of Chairman Mao* (1994)—could indulge in sensual pleasures, keeping an entourage of concubines, mistresses and simple girls. The poor and the weak, on the other hand, had to be content with an extremely ascetic life. While the man had the license to sow his wild oats, the woman had to preserve her chastity by observing a very strict moral code of behavior.

The sexual exploitation and repression of women was symbolized by the high and tight collars they had to wear, and by the 1000-year-old political institution of foot-binding which could, it was believed, increase her sexual charm. It was also thought to ensure her chastity by confining her social circles within the threshold.

The subject of class and gender repression of women has been explored by many, modern Chinese writers, e.g., Lu Xun, particularly in his short story, "New Year's Eve."[1] It was also utilized as a powerful political weapon by the Communists during the Chinese Civil War, to call upon the poor and down-trodden to rise up against the ruling class. A dramatic example can be seen in the opera, "The White-haired Girl."[2]

Thus, reading Hardy, in terms of his treatment of sexual morality in *Tess of the d'Urbervilles, Return of the Native, Jude the Obscure* as well as *A Pair of Blue Eyes*, would be relevant both historically and culturally. It would have a subversive effect on the Confucian hierarchy and double-standard which was officially condemned at the beginning of the modern era, but is still practiced by the rich and the powerful, as Mao did behind the forbidden red walls. It had also remained deep-

NOTES: 1. "New Year's Eve:" a short story by Lu Xun in which a young widow goes to work as a domestic servant for a rich family, loses her only son to wolves, and is later kidnapped and forced into another marriage. After the second husband dies, she comes back to serve the same family and eventually is fired for fear that her loss of chastity will bring ill luck. Troubled by the prospect of two husbands fighting for her in the afterlife and tortured by poverty, she dies during the night of a snowstorm.

2. "The White-haired Girl:" a popular opera during the Chinese Civil War period (1945–49). Xi'er is forced to work as a domestic servant for a rich landlord to pay back the debt left by her father who had committed suicide. After being raped by the landlord, she runs into the mountains, gives birth to a baby and buries it alive. Living on nothing but wild fruit, her hair eventually turns white, and she is taken to be a ghost by the villagers.

rooted in the mass culture, as was manifested in the widespread female infanticides in rural areas.

Paradoxically, such a reading in the China of the 1980s, though more liberalized than before, would still have to fit itself into the measurements of the orthodox literary ideology. Angel, Henry, their preferences and the murderous social environment surrounding Sue and Jude would by necessity have to be explained, explicitly or implicitly, as testimonies of bourgeois and petty bourgeois hypocrisy. This hypocrisy, it has to be pointed out, was either absent or had been eliminated in the socialist New China, just as the tragedy of the white-haired girl could only happen in the old China before 1949. Ironically, reading Hardy for its moral and political subversiveness would be impractical both historically and culturally.

Deviating from the orthodox course for literature study, I decided to take a less political path. I wanted to be faithful to the overflow of powerful emotional responses I experienced in reading Hardy's novels. I saw in Hardy's tragedies the destruction of beauty through a loss of balance between the *Yin* and *Yang* principles, in the unfolding dramas of the trios of Tess, Angel, and Alec; Eustacia, Clym, and Wildeve; Elfride, Stephen, and Henry; and Jude, Sue, and Arabella. The scales were tipped by a blind force which draws its life from a multiplicity of sources—personal, social and supernatural—and indulges in sporting with the fates of these characters.

The inquiry into my emotional responses eventually evolved into the main contention of my master's thesis: Hardy's major novels can produce pity and fear, and effect the proper purgation of these emotions, as conceptualized by Aristotle, through a successful reconciliation of the tragic ideal, traditionally identified with classic tragedies, with the modern novel which is biased genetically towards realism.

While working on the thesis, I traveled to universities in Beijing, Shanghai and other big cities to gather whatever secondary sources were available pertaining to my topic. At Fudan University in Shanghai, I happened upon the index card for Dale Kramer's *Thomas Hardy: The Forms of Tragedy* (1975). Excited, I checked with the librarian who kindly informed me that the book was in the hands of another graduate student in the English Department.

In a typical Chinese way, I was introduced to that student through a mutual friend. When I walked into his dorm, I spotted the book right away on his brownish wicker bookshelf, but was denied access to it because he wanted to use it for his own thesis. Because of a plagiarism complication later, however, he was not granted the privilege to do a thesis at all.

I did not realize how behind I was with my Hardy studies until I came to Illinois State in the spring of 1989. That semester, I was privileged to be a research assistant to a respected Hardy scholar, Dr. William Morgan. During our first meeting, I mentioned my master's thesis and apologized for my not-so-up-to-date knowledge of Hardy, citing in passing the unhappy Fudan anecdote. Good-humoredly, Morgan picked up a book from one of his ceiling-touching shelves and said, "Here is your Kramer."

Five years had elapsed since I completed my master's studies and, counting the date Kramer's book was published, I was more than 10 years behind.

Morgan became interested in the thesis and, in spite my profuse apologies not only out of Chinese modesty, but also out of a heartfelt feeling of its unworthiness, he insisted that I bring the thesis to him. A week later, he returned my thesis with generous comments about the "grace and clarity" of my writing, the "thoroughness" with which I pursued the thesis, and the "narrative authenticity" I established by allowing the fact that I admire Hardy, and that I am moved by his work, to show through.

Notwithstanding, he reconfirmed my fear that my study "is a little dated by Western standards," because "people aren't as interested in Hardy the tragedian now as they used to be in the U. S. and U. K.," and I would probably have trouble trying to publish it here. With a sensitivity typical of Morgan, he quickly added, "but still, it's very well done, and you need not be troubled by its not being precisely what we're doing over here: it stands on its own merits."

But the reality of my "datedness" was soon brought home to me in the graduate seminars. That very semester, I learned, the hard way, that the discourse of literary studies in the West, had in the last couple of decades, without my witnessing, undergone revolutionary changes. The whole range of humanistic assumptions, from subjectivity to authorship to textuality, had been questioned if not dismantled.

The concept of realism, which I invoked in my apology for Hardy, as a modern tragedian writing in the form of novel, had been challenged as epistemologically naîve. My first position paper in a seminar on Shakespeare was roundly "attacked" by my fellow graduate students who, it seemed to me, were caught in a rage against anything not fitting the procrustean bed of postmodernism. The very topic of my paper, the paradoxical nature of Othello's character, seemed to them so hopelessly nineteenth-century. Not until the professor—who, amused, had withdrawn in his mobile chair to a distant corner of the room as the "slaughter" began—came to my rescue, did I finally succeed in fighting my way out of the "siege."

While I was paying close attention to what was happening on the Tiananmen Square that first semester, a lot was going on in my seminar on the 19th Century English Novel. Indeed, the seminar seemed more like a battlefield, especially to one who had been used to the quiet, non-confrontational and decorous classroom of my native country. It was a shouting match between students, and between students and the professor, also a distinguished scholar in Victorian literature.

The topic of the course was the fallen woman, which we traced from Eve and Helen, all the way down to Tess. Exciting as it certainly was, the seminar was also unsettling. While I was sympathetic to the feministic reading pursued by my fellow students, I found many of them letting themselves be carried away by their enthusiasm. They seemed so bent on seeing a rapist, real or potential, or at least a misogynist in every male character in the novels we were reading, that they became impatient with, or contemptuous of, textual and contextual evidences. The politically charged rhetoric provoked memories of the Cultural Revolution, and reminded me of the dogmatic Marxist literary criticisms I had read before, and of political study sessions I had happily left behind.

A debate on whether Tess was raped or seduced in the late 1990s would seem so anachronistic because in most states today the use of force does not have to be involved in deciding what is considered rape. Back in the spring of 1989, however, we, being pedantic, had to fight to the very end over the fine distinctions. My argument was that it was impossible to deliver the verdict that Tess was raped, without a reasonable doubt, largely because of the authorial ambivalence, and the profound silence the narrator kept at every critical moment in the story.

Hardy's ambivalence and silence in this novel are proverbial and need not bother us here. Tess's loss of balance, however, was manifested in her being attracted to Alec physically, despite herself, and her rejecting him on a spiritual level. She rejects Alec because of her independent spirit and her awareness of the coarseness of Alec, which is betrayed by his "swarthy complexion with full lips," his pointed mustache, and his "bold rolling eye." But those "touches of barbarism" are not without their mesmeric masculine charm for a young, inexperienced yet sensitive girl. So she would "blush" under that bold stare, and, obeying "like one in a dream," eat in a "half-pleased, half-reluctant" state whatever Alec put in her mouth. Since whatever actually happened in the Chase scene is buried in the deliberate authorial silence, I argued, based upon the by-now-obsolete distinction between rape and seduction in terms of the use of violence or force, that Tess might have been seduced at the level of her physical being, and raped spiritually. I also contended that Hardy's ambivalence, and indeed the rich variety of portraits of women in Victorian literature, angel in the house, the fallen woman, the wronged woman, or the fortunate fall, deflates the myth of a coherent, consistent Victorian morality.

Whatever thesis was drawn in that seminar only dissolved into antithesis. We parted, agreeing to disagree. I felt at the time that I had had enough with Hardy. I "defected." I decided to work on something else for my doctoral dissertation. But there has always been a soft spot in my heart for Old Hardy. Is it due to the memories of my overflowing emotional responses when I stumbled upon Hardy? Is it because it is hard for me to forget the "squares climbing" on many a hot and sweaty Nanjing summer night? Is it because, even today, I can smell the intoxicatingly fresh print when my first papers on Hardy were published? Or is it for the simple fact that the world Hardy created still has a firm grip on my imagination?

P. S.: Whether a half-hearted or whole-hearted Hardy fan, I recently completed a translation of another of his novels: *The Well-Beloved*. The chief-editor at the same press told me that they are already at the typesetting stage.

I only hope, though, that this time around the labor and birth will not be as suspenseful.

Why Do These Flowers Blooming Inside the Garden Seem More ?

Receptions of Contemporary Chinese Films at Home and Abroad

APRIL, 1997

THERE IS A PROVERBIAL SAYING in Chinese which goes: *qiang nei kai hua qiang wai xiang*. It translates as, "flowers blooming luxuriantly inside the garden walls seem more fragrant to passersby outside." It seems to be an apt description of the different receptions contemporary Chinese films have encountered at home and abroad.

Before the end of the 80s, few if any in the West had ever heard of Chinese films. Since the *Yellow Earth* (1984), the harbinger of the fifth generation of directors, however, Chinese movies have burst upon the world cinematic scenes with splendor and carried away one award after another: Gold Bear for the *Red Sorghum* at the Berlin Film Festival (1988), Academy Award Nomination for Best Foreign Language Film for *Ju Dou* (1990), the same honor for *Raise The Red Lantern* (1991), The Best Actress Award for *The Story of Qiu Ju* at the 1992 Venice Film Festival. Besides the Academy Award Nomination for Best Foreign Language Film, *Farewell, My Concubine* (1993) claimed the Golden Globe as the Best Foreign Film and the Best Picture honors at the Cannes Film Festival. And many more.

Reviewers and critics have lavished praise upon these films: "lushly and breathtakingly filmed," "extraordinary," "one of the most beautiful," "a gorgeous fable," "an exotic oriental treasure," "imposingly beautiful," "fabulously pictorial," "spectacularly vast," and on, and on.

Back at home, however, it has been quite a different story. *Red Sorghum* did enjoy phenomenal success. Indeed, many of us can still howl a few notes from the song screamed out by the male sedan-carrier protagonist at the top of his hoarse voice before the abduction and seduction of the young bride in the wild sorghum fields: "Sis, don't you be shy and look behind you, just walk on. . . " But most of the other films have experienced one kind of trouble or another: either they've been censored, banned or simply given a cold shoulder.

When I went to the movie theater during my visit to China in the summer of 1995, I had a difficult time finding any Chinese movie to see. I did get to see *Shanghai Triad* in Shanghai, but the film—which won the Academy Award Nomination for Best Achievement in Cinematography, and was hailed as the best foreign film by the National Board of Review and the LA and NY film critics circles—didn't seem to attract a big and enthusiastic crowd. Flooding the screens everywhere were such Hollywood hits as *True Lies, Toy Story, Speed, Lion King,* and *Forrest Gump.* When these shows were not playing, the theater was, to use a Chinese idiom, *men ke luo que,* meaning "at the entrance of the movie theaters you could set up a net to catch sparrows." In other words, it would be completely deserted.

It was much the same during my visit during the summer of 1996.

A ready explanation for the difference in popularity could be the tight, ideological control that manifests itself as paranoiac censorship in mainland China. I would argue that while ideological control is the most conspicuous culprit here, there are many more complex and subtle cultural factors at work which deserve our careful, critical attention.

There is no doubt that those films which have been successful abroad are worth every penny of those epithets: "lushly and breathtakingly filmed," "fabulously pictorial," "spectacularly vast," and "imposingly beautiful." But the beauty is of a perverse and twisted kind. Indeed, if there is anything which can unify them all, it is poverty, backwardness and battered humanity.

The Yellow Earth (dir. by Chen Kaige, 1984) is a story about a village girl in the late 1930s, who has been pre-arranged to marry a man who is much older, and whom she doesn't love. But the real protagonist is the yellow earth which stretches endlessly and timelessly: barren, scorched and hostile.

Near the end of the movie, the girl, after fulfilling her duty to her family by marrying the older man, comes back and takes a tiny boat across the violent and roaring muddy currents of the Yellow River towards her new life. But the viewer is left hanging in a heart-breaking uncertainty: Did she make it, or was she swallowed up by the malicious, yellow currents? It's on the same vast, barren yellow earth that the epic drama of *Life On a String* (dir. by Chen Kaige, 1991) was played. On this boundless, physical and spiritual wasteland, humans are like swarms of tiny insects caught in a perennial, bloody feud against each other. Trekking across this desert are an aged minstrel-saint and his young apprentice, both blind, in search of salvation and sight. As expected, the young apprentice's budding love for a peasant girl ends in tragedy, and the minstrel-saint, a would-be Chinese Moses, fails to find sight for himself, or to lead his people out of their subjection to superstition, ignorance, intolerance and inhumanity.

The same perversity dominates *Raise the Red Lantern* (dir. by Zhang Yimou, 1991), a movie set in 1920s China. Here, the somewhat college educated 19 year-old Songlian is sucked into a rivalry among several wives of the same master. A would-be new woman, she is quickly reduced to a narrow-minded and manipulating freak, ending up with the deaths of two other twisted creatures, like herself, on her hands.

In the family dye mill of *Ju Dou* (dir. by Zhang Yimou, 1991), an old impotent and miserly husband sadistically abuses his young wife and drives her into the arms of his harshly exploited and sexually repressed nephew. But the fruit of that semi-incestuous love proves to be too bitter: their half-witted son eventually kills nearly everybody involved, and burns the family mill down.

One finds the same type of insanity in almost all the other films, *Farewell, My Concubine* (dir. by Chen Kaige, 1993), *The Blue Kite* (dir. by Tian Zhuangzhuang, 1993), *Red Sorghum* (dir. by Zhang Yimou, 1987), *The Day The Sun Turned Cold* (dir. Yim Ho, 1994) in one way or another.

All these powerful cinematic representations of Chinese life are historically accurate.

Even Mao Zedong himself, back in 1942 in his "Talks on Art and Literature" in Yenan, recognized that there are dark sides to life that need to be exposed. However, art and literature, he decreed, must be fit "properly into the whole revolutionary machine as one of its component parts" and they should be used as "a powerful weapon for uniting and educating the people" so that China might "fight the enemy with one heart and one mind." This decree has been upheld as the classic guideline for literature in China ever since, though it has been interpreted according to circumstances.

There is nothing wrong with using literature for political purpose. To perform *The White-haired Girl* for the soldiers before a major battle, in order to work up their morale, is not much different from the inspirational gospel singing the night before the last bayonet-fighting in the Hollywood hit *Glory*, a favorite of mine that I have watched many times. A line should be drawn, though, when literature is employed solely as a handmaid or pageboy in the political arena. This has often been the case in China.

In 1951, Mao penned an editorial in the *People's Daily* blasting the movie *Wu Xun Zhuan*, which started a campaign to educate writers and artists, politically. In 1954, Mao threw his political weight into a literary debate between a young scholar, Li Xifang, and his mentor, Yu Ping-po over the classic novel *Dream of the Red Chamber*, which started a national campaign to criticize Yu Ping-po, Hu Shi and eventually Hu Feng, and the more extensive purge of "bourgeois thought" in literature and art.

The Hundred Flowers Movement in 1956, meant to give artists and writers greater freedom, quickly turned into a brutal Anti-rightists movement. In 1965, at Mao's prodding, Wu Han's play *Hai Rei Ba Guan (Hai Rui's Dismissal)* was denounced. Soon, it became clear that this literary debate was the prelude to a ten-year nightmare during the Cultural Revolution.

In 1975, Mao invited a few literary scholars to his study to discuss the classic novel *Shuihuzhuan (Water Margin)*. This discussion once again turned the wheel of political fortune against Deng Xiaoping.

It would be hard for writers and artists, who are under the absolute protection of the First Amendment on this side of the Pacific, to really appreciate this master-servant relationship between politics and literature. To tamper with freedom of expression in any form or manner in the U. S. would only invite trouble for oneself. Dan Quayle found this out in 1992 when he lambasted the TV character Murphy Brown for having a baby outside of wedlock. I wonder what he has to say to Ellen DeGeneres' "coming out" openly as a gay star.

The most the U. S. government can do is to put pressure on the TV industry and Hollywood to self-regulate, or else resort to the magic V-Chip. Tipper Gore and concerned parents have already successfully pressured the music industry to put warning labels on explicit or controversial CDs. For the Chinese government, though, the scissors are mightier, and much more convenient.

Why Do These Flowers Blooming Inside the Garden Walls... 189

It would take more than a stretch of imagination for the censors in China to find those internationally successful Chinese films uplifting because they do not seem to serve the all-exclusive goal in the post-Mao era: to tap to the fullest potential of people's enthusiasm to build the Four Modernizations. Dwelling on the past, digging deep into the wounds, being obsessed with poverty, backwardness, "kinky" hetero- and homosexual behavior, in their eyes, in no way boosts the morale of the people. It could even work to shake people's confidence in the political structure of the country. Even though sexually-explicit scenes in such films as *Ju Dou* are tame by Western standards, they, according to Liu, a censor at the ministry of culture, are "a bad influence on the physical and spiritual health of young people." Government workers like Liu consider themselves moral guardians of the nation. So applying the scissors falls well within their noble responsibility.

But to blame it all on the censorship is only to point out the obvious, and to oversimplify a very complex cultural as well as political phenomenon.

Since almost all of those award-winning films dig into the moral, cultural and political wounds of China, one of the first questions we should ask, beyond an obvious political discussion, should be: Are Chinese viewers ready for a long, hard look deep inside themselves, and their past?

Take *Farewell, My Concubine*. Jenny Kwok Wah Lau, in a well-informed and insightful study of the film, regards it as a melodrama because of its artistic and political compromises. One such compromise, according to Lau, is the alteration of the ending: instead of letting Dieyi and Xiaolou leave mainland China after the Cultural Revolution and reside in Hong Kong, as in the original novel, Dieyi commits suicide in the film while playing Yu Ji the Concubine to Xiaolou, as Xian Yu the Conqueror, one last time.

But this alteration not only fits Dieyi's character, with his uncompromising but twisted sense of fidelity both to art and to life, but it also brings the drama to a perfect and tragic ending. This movie may be melodramatic, but I believe it is a powerful study of human nature or at least of Chinese character.

But are the Chinese audiences ready for such thorough tragedies? Are they ready for such painful probing into their own character? The Chinese people, according to Dr. Zhu Guangqian, in his dissertation on *Tragic Pleasure* (1933), lack the thoroughly tragic spirit that characterizes their European counterparts. They are one of the most practical and pragmatic people in the world. *Zhi zu zhe chang le,* to be content is to be happy, is their philosophy. To achieve and maintain a level of equilibrium, even in times of hardship, is a mark of moral strength. They tend not to wrack their brains about issues which do not immediately concern themselves. There is a certain degree of fatalism in their world outlook that leads to a resignation: to destiny and to optimism, instead of pessimism.

Thus, classic Chinese tragedies are, arguably, never real tragedies in the Western sense of the term. No matter how much pity and fear they arouse through characters' sufferings, there is almost always a happy ending to cheer the audience up: either a righteous emperor, or official, arrives in the final scene to punish evil, and bring justice as in *The Tragedy of Dou Er*; or lovers, destroyed in this world, are reunited in a dreamland or the afterlife as in the well-known Chinese *Romeo and Juliet: Liangshan Bo and Zhu Yingtai,* otherwise known as The *Butterfly Lovers.*

If the tragedy of Dieyi, Xiaolou and Juixian in *Farewell, My Concubine* extends through several important historical periods—post Xinhai Revolution (1911) years, War of Resistance Against Japan, Civil War between the Nationalists and Communists, all the way to the Cultural Revolution in the late 1960s—its root causes, logically, lie deeper than Communist rule. It would not be too far-fetched to say that theirs is not only a personal tragedy or a political tragedy, but more significantly, a Chinese tragedy, a tragedy of Chinese culture and national character.

Last year, I watched a panel discussion on a major network, marking the 20th anniversary of the Cultural Revolution. On the question of whether such a tragedy would ever occur again, all the panelists—Chinese scholars on this subject—rightly cited the current less-than-democratic political system as fertile soil for that evil flower to germinate, bud, and bloom again. But to my great disappointment, none of the panelists reached deeper into the national character for the root cause. It is much easier to blame it all on Mao and the Gang of Four, than to face our own share of the collective guilt.

For the same reasons, it would be difficult for both the government and audiences to feel uplifted by films such as *Farewell, My Concubine.* For them, the all-encompassing priority is to seize the day and seize the moment to modernize, to make a splash or at least get wet in the "sea of commerce."

Who can afford the luxury of stopping to nurse wounds, or poke beneath scars? What about the majority of people who cannot "make a splash?" or "get wet?" They can maintain a level of equilibrium by meditating the *zhi zu zhe chang le* philosophy, or by indulging nostalgically in memory of the "good old days," including the Cultural Revolution days. This might account for the "Red Sun" whirlwind across China a few years ago where we witnessed the resurrection of Mao hymns and revolutionary march songs.

Anyone of us, forty-something and older, who has howled in a karaoke club back in China recently knows what I am talking about. You know the lyrics are often silly and nonsensical, but you scream them out at the top of your lungs anyway. You experience a queer, bittersweet feeling, shivering with goose bumps all over your body. You are, for the moment, reliving your childhood, your lost youth, and your shattered dreams. The total effect is cathartic or even orgasmic, if I may.

Another trait in Chinese culture and in its national character, which affects the popularity of these films, is the "no dirty linen in public" mentality. While the Chinese do not have an monopoly of this mentality, their humiliating experiences with foreign powers since the Opium War, the fact that almost all of these films have been funded by outside money, and have won awards by parading the "dirty linen" on international screens, make them more leery of the motives behind those awards. It doesn't matter much that the closet holding the linen is virtually translucent anyway.

The same mentality, right or wrong, has affected China's handling of Tibet, Hong Kong and other issues where Chinese pride and sovereignty are perceived to be at stake.

I am not going to follow the quasi-scientific labeling of Chinese as a "shame culture" in comparison to the "guilt culture" of Western civilizations. Studies have shown that structures of guilt and shame are quite similar across cultures, owing to the possibly universal societal functions of these two feelings. Without these feelings holding people back, the world would be filled with unconscionable liars, cheats, fakers and petty thieves, to say the least.

There is disagreement concerning the exact distinctions between shame and guilt. Some even question whether they are distinct feelings at all. Most scholars, however, seem to agree that shame "arises from tension between the ego and the ego-ideal, and is usually accompanied by a sense of personal inadequacy and failure," and by "apprehension of an evaluation by an external audience," whereas guilt is "experienced whenever an emotionally charged barrier erected by the superego is touched or transgressed; it is, in other words, conceived as a form of internal sanction mediated by an individual's conscience."

Without getting into the debate of whether Chinese culture is one of shame or guilt, it is not too far off to say that Chinese viewers can very well recognize in their culture, and in their own character, the "inadequacies" portrayed in those films. Consequently, while they may be elated by the awards from abroad, they are painfully aware of the fact that these awards are won at the heavy cost of parading shameful Chinese linen in front of foreign audiences.

No wonder those films sparked fierce debates within Chinese intellectual circles, on the mainland and abroad, particularly over their success in the West. Many suspected that those films were made to cater to the taste buds of Western critics and audiences. One of the young writers of the emotionally charged *China Can Say No* (1996) complains, with obvious sarcasm, that "Chinese movie-makers have mastered the art of turning the yellow earth and rags into beauty, and making trash in Chinese culture more ugly and more evil."

Dan Yang, who is teaching women's literature in the U. S., denounces *Raise the Red Lantern* as a porno that provides "sexual appetizers for rich, white males in the West." It is, Dan Yang goes on to pronounce, "a castration, an insult and a betrayal of all Chinese, Chinese women in particular."

Even Dai Qing, a prominent dissident journalist who has been highly critical of Chinese government, concludes in a raging article on *Raise the Red Lantern* that "this kind of film is really shot for the casual pleasures of foreigners." She calls on the Chinese audiences not to "close their eyes" to Zhang Yimou's artistic dishonesty "just because they dislike the hardliners in Beijing."

Many a critic who once defended these moviemakers have had a change of heart. They now denounce Zhang and his like as "a group of overrated, callow and pretentious self-promoters." Some of these criticisms may taste of sour grapes. Just recall such old Chinese axioms as *wen ren xian qing*, men of letters look down upon each other, or *tong hang shi yuan jia*, men of the same trade are natural enemies, or listen to this anecdote reported in a Shanghai tabloid publication.

Before *Farewell, My Concubine* brought him showers of critical accolades from abroad, Chen Kaige once went into the lavatory with a newspaper article announcing a major prize Zhang Yimou had just won, and didn't emerge until almost an hour later, cursing: "He's a fucking cameraman, *my* cameraman!" Zhang was his cinematographer when he was making the *Yellow Earth*.

We could go on exploring why the flowers do not seem fragrant to those inside the garden walls—the rise of popular culture, the change in audiences' taste buds, market factors, etc.— but it is time to turn to examine the other half of the issue: Why do they seem so fragrant to people outside the garden walls?

Again, there is no easy answer. However, some of the reviews by the media in this country may offer an index: *Washington Post* called *Farewell, My Concubine* "lavish, splendorous, ornate." The *Los Angeles Times* found it "gorgeous and intoxicating." *Newsweek* hailed it as "a cinematic grand slam" and The *New York Times* extolled it as "one of those very rare film spectacles that deliver just about everything." The most telling comments would come from *Playboy*. It promotes *Farewell, My Concubine* as an "exotic story of love and betrayal" and *Raise the Red Lantern* as "an exotic oriental treasure."

This fascination with the Orient, particularly the mystifying China, may go as far back as the first and second centuries AD, when Rome at its height sought the elegant silks of China transported by caravan from Changan to Antioch on the Mediterranean along the tortuous "Silk Road." It surely goes back to the first direct contact between Europe and Asia in the 13th century when China, under the Mongol Yuan dynasty (1260–1368 AD) opened its doors to outside travelers like the Venetian Marco Polo, who in his reports described admiringly the resplendent court of Kublai Khan, the people, and the countryside.

American colonists got their first impressions of China from England, but after the colonies gained independence, American ships ventured to the Far East directly, carrying ginseng and furs from the Pacific Northwest, sandalwood from the Hawaiian Islands, and later, opium from Turkey as mediums of exchange. They brought home cargoes of Chinese products. Direct exposure to the visual art and crafts of China gave Americans their first and, for many, their only knowledge of that distant land. The image formed was one of a "fantastic, uncivilized nation of strange people who lived on the opposite side of the globe, a fitting location for such a weird society."

In the subsequent decades through the Opium War, the Boxer Uprising, the Second World War, the Chinese Civil War, the Cultural Revolution, all the way to the post-Tiananmen Square years, the fascination with China will remain even though its ingredients have been a changing mixture of admiration, pity, suspicion and raw contempt. Admiration for the splendor of this ancient civilization. Pity for this sleeping giant when she was trampled upon by her much smaller neighbor and other foreign powers. Contempt for the sickly, poverty-stricken "heathen Chinese." And suspicion as to what the giant will do when she finally wakes up—just listen to the chorus of the so-called "China threat."

When the *Yellow Earth* and other films made by China's fifth generation of movie-makers hit the international cinematic scene, it was the first time its ancient culture, people, and land were brought home to Europeans and Americans through mesmerizing sound and images made by Chinese themselves. These images, understandably, are much more fresh and authentic than the thoroughly diabolical image of Fu Manchu, a brilliant but mad scientist and arch villain, who appealed to the American public in the first Fu Manchu movie in 1929, to its newest version as recently as 1981. These images are more fresh and authentic than the more favorable and human, but condescendingly portrayed Charlie Chan (1925–1932), the Hawaiian-based detective. Even more fresh and authentic than the sympathetic portrayal by Pearl Buck in her Nobel-Prize winning novel *Good Earth* (1931), who, regrettably, makes her rustic, semi-illiterate peasants speak in polished, elegant prose with complex syntactic structures.

Suddenly, China had stripped herself unashamedly before the bold eye of the West, exposing all her beauty and ugliness. Who could not help but fall in love?

Especially when such beauty and ugliness were seen through Zhang Yimou's often "razor sharp" lens, and delivered by Chen Kaige's grand, poetic, epic-style cinematography. Most of Zhang's *Qiu Ju*, for instance, was filmed in a village so remote that the production crew had to use portable, electric generators. Much of the action was shot with concealed cameras, sometimes filming through holes in walls. Besides Gong Li, *Qiu Ju* has only three professional performers: the actors who play her husband, the village chief, and the local police officer. In making *Life on a String*, Chen Kaige wanted to show the landscape "not just as backdrop, but as a

Why Do These Flowers Blooming Inside the Garden Walls... 195

spiritual world." So the camera was always panning up, exploring, searching." The landscape became as much a protagonist as the blind minstrel-saint.

However, mere freshness, novelty and cinematographic experimentation would not have been enough to win over the Western audiences. What was needed was appropriate subject matter. Ironically, appropriate subject matter seems to be comprised of the taboos or unmentionables of the social and political life of Chinese people.

Western critics have liked the way Zhang—ever since *Red Sorghum*—applies his "ravishing cinematography to his favorite themes: sex, lies, violence, and power." They see subversive political symbolism in almost every one of these films: the leprous, old man who bought the young bride in *Red Sorghum*; the miserly, sadistic, impotent old husband and stern-looking patriarchs in *Judo;* the faceless master in *Raise the Red Lantern* who manipulates the four wives and plays them off against each other, etc.—all of these can be read as disguised criticism of gerontocratic (septuagenarian or octogenarian) politics in China.

Commenting on *Life on a String*, Chen Kaige says, "when the villagers beat up a boy in a scene near the end, I had to conjure up Tiananmen Square. But, of course, you can't express that directly, you have to be oblique." And the scenes of clan warfare, he adds, have echoes of the infamous Cultural Revolution. "My father was a film director at the time when cinema in China just stopped. Only propaganda films were made, and no films from other countries could be seen. The people now realize that the Cultural Revolution was a big tragedy."

The Cultural Revolution is not really taboo in China. In fact, there have been many films and TV series on this subject directly and indirectly. What makes a movie like *Farewell, My Concubine* "subversive" is that the protagonists seem to suffer more during the Cultural Revolution than they do in the hands of the Kuomingtang, the Japanese invaders, and debauched eunuchs of the Qing Dynasty.

Indeed, such films offer Western reviewers and critics ample opportunity to do what they do best: deconstruct and psychoanalyze. Take *The Day the Sun Turned Cold*: winner of Best Film and Best Director at the 1991 Tokyo Film Festival.

In this rich and complex mystery story based on an actual Chinese criminal case, Guan Jin, a young welder living in a northern province of China, accuses his own mother of poisoning his father to death ten years before. To critics who are versed in psychoanalytic approaches to art and literature, it is a "brilliant exploration of Oedipal love and betrayal." If there is anything Oedipal in this movie, it must have escaped me. To me, it is a powerful drama of Guan Jin being torn between his sense of justice, and his love for his dead father on the one hand, and his love for his mother on the other.

For Pleasure, a movie directed by Ning Ying about the "comic-dramatic tribulations of a group of pensioners who devote their energy to reviving the Beijing Opera," has been interpreted as a "subtle metaphor for the Chinese gerontocracy." Gerontocratic China may be concerned with the preservation of such endangered species as Chinese traditional and folk art forms, but I doubt Chinese audiences are. I don't think they would be inclined to see any political symbolism or subtext in such a movie.

Do Western reviewers and critics tend to read too much into these films? Responding to comments that *Raise the Red Lantern* symbolizes a power struggle within the Chinese leadership, Zhang Yimou responds: "I'm not sure what it—struggle, *dou*—symbolizes. You can associate it with the course of Chinese history, which is a whole series of fighting and struggle. We can associate it with the way different countries behave; every country finds a reason to fight another country. In terms of human history, there has never been any peace. It's just like our story: everyone fights each other, and in the end, every one dies. It's meaningless. This story has a kind of universality; it not only refers to our own country but to the human situation. It grows from all these symbols, from all these associations. You don't have to confine it just to China. . . "

As to culturally specific references in these films, I have found that many viewers in the U.S., even well educated ones, do not seem to have the basic historical knowledge to really appreciate such Chinese films. Take, for example, *The Joy Luck Club*, a popular Hollywood movie. Many of my friends who have seen it, fail—understandably—to pick up the cues which place the flashbacks of the four mothers in the years of the War of Resistance Against Japan, or the Chinese Civil War before 1949.

The polyphonic structure of *Farewell, My Concubine* may prove to be even more inaccessible. This may sound condescending, but I don't know how many of those glowing reviewers and critics can really appreciate the intricate inter-

Why Do These Flowers Blooming Inside the Garden Walls... 197

relations between the historical story of Chu Ba Wang—*Chu the Conqueror* (232–303 BC), and Yu Ju-Yu the Concubine in *Farewell, My Concubine*—the popular Beijing Opera of the tragic love story between Chu and Yu, and the tragic story of Dieyi, Xiaolou and Ju Xian in the 20th century, or the unfolding of the tragedy against changing historical backdrops.

One might even go so far as to say that the success of recent Chinese films in the West owes much to the birth of a Chinese star who offers an exotic charm different from that of Jodie Foster, Sharon Stone or Demi Moore. Reviewers find Gong Li "chastely glamorous, achingly beautiful" in *Red Sorghum*, and "demure and passionate, exploited and rebellious" in *Ju Dou* and *Raise the Red Lantern* (1991). To them, it's almost a pity that in *Qiu Ju*, Gong Li has to cover her shapely body with those thick, unsightly country clothes.

However, the statement that films by Zhang Yimou, Chen Kaige and a few other Chinese directors in the last decade or so have been very popular needs to be modified. They have been popular only to the degree that no Chinese films have ever made it to the popular screen or to Blockbuster in the West, not even to mention winning so many awards. Their popularity is limited to Chinese and Asian communities, to Academia (e.g., among humanities professors), to people who are in the business of reviewing and critiquing films and to a few other Sinophiles.

The reason is simple and obvious: Americans by and large are not really interested in foreign films, or in what's going on in the world, for that matter. When I visited China the last couple of summers, my old friends, even those who didn't go to college, could talk to me about American society, election politics, Clinton, etc. somewhat knowledgeably, even though their information may have been censored. But in my college classrooms in the U.S.—I have been teaching in this country since 1989—I have seen very few students who show a genuine interest in, and can really discuss, broad international issues, let alone particular subjects like the Middle East or China, intelligently. This assessment may sound harsh and no more than anecdotal, but I have found it to be increasingly true.

According to a recent article in *Time* titled "Fellini Go Home!" by Richard Corliss, America has "scant appreciation" for directors who work in foreign languages. In fact, 1996's earnings of foreign language films amounted to less than 1 % of the total U.S. box office. "I love these films and want to support them," says Bingham Ray of October Films, "but it's a real uphill struggle. You feel like Sisyphus. . . the sad fact is that foreign-language films no longer matter. Americans, absorbed in their junk culture, are shuttering a window to the rest of the movie world. . .Don't wanna read; don't wanna see. . .Bosnia and Rwanda—big yawn. The real problem is our boredom with anything outside ourselves." "More and more," says Tom Brueggemann, who books specialized cinematic fare for Loews Theaters, "Americans are obsessively and exclusively interested in American culture. Even college students now tend to like the same films everyone else likes. If they have niche tastes, it's not for Bergman and Bunuel but for Beavis and Butthead."

Of course, not all college students are bored with things outside themselves. Upset by Corliss's alleged Generation X bashing, a junior at Carnegie Mellon University responds: "Hey dude, listen up. As a junior at Carnegie Mellon University, I am offended by such a blanket statement. Believe it or not, there are mature, intelligent college students who can understand, follow and appreciate foreign films. We can even grasp all the topics that gramps knew."

Another college student, offended but unapologetic, complains that "subtitles turn a movie into a job. Dubbing just sounds phony. If writers and directors choose to work in languages other than English, fine. But don't belittle me for staying home."

I'd like to conclude with this tantalizing question: Can flowers blooming in Chinese gardens smell just as fragrant to those inside as to those outside?

The example of Zhang Yu, an award-winning-actress-turned-U.S.-educated director, seems to offer a thread of hope. Critical of moviemakers who were obsessed with China's past, poverty, etc., Zhang has directed a movie titled *The Solar Fire* which focuses on the life of a female entrepreneur and her struggle since the 1980s. Set in cosmopolitan Beijing and Shanghai, it won the Best Film Award at Berlin Film Festival in 1996 without parading dirty Chinese linen, or projecting subversive political symbolism. Zhang, the producer, scriptwriter, lead actress as well as director of the movie, is very optimistic that the movie will be very popular with Chinese audiences.

I can not wait to check it out for myself.

Hubris and Humility:
Is There A Happy Mean?

MARCH, 1998

NOT TOO LONG AGO, a local radio talk show was giving young people free tickets to a concert. All you needed to do was call and play a musical instrument on the radio. This mother called in and got her 12-year-old daughter to the phone with her violin. From the very first note, I knew my day was ruined: it was not any more musical than the nerve-racking squawking made by a chicken being chased by a naughty puppy, and I had a hard time shaking it out of my eardrums for the rest of the day.

When the acoustic torture was over, the mother cheered: "Isn't she wonderful? Isn't she wonderful?" For a second, even the always nice, warm and enthusiastic deejays found themselves tongue-tied. "How long has your daughter been taking violin lessons?" they recovered right away. "Four years. Isn't she wonderful?!" answered the proud mother.

This reminded me of the early summer of 1981 on the breathtakingly beautiful campus of Beijing University. The Fulbright program (one of the first such cultural exchange programs run in China after it reopened its doors to the outside world) was just over, and we were all excited. We were shamelessly anxious to find out how the gray-haired, distinguished-looking American professor was going to evaluate us. "You're *the best* student I've ever taught. . . ," one of us tore open his report and read aloud proudly.

His joy proved premature. "You're *the very best* I've ever taught. . . ," another of us was congratulated by the same venerable professor. Which was quickly challenged by another announcement in another report. "You're *by far the best* I've ever taught. . . "

We were confused, scratching our heads. Who was *really* the best?

A few years later, in a graduate seminar on Shakespeare during my first semester in the States, I wrote a paper on the paradoxical nature of Othello's character. At the end of a heated discussion (among a group of "cocky neurotics," to borrow from Vladimir Nabokov) on the paper, the professor, his well-trimmed whiskers quivering, his eyes sparkling with humor, declared to the conclave that my paper was "an *excellent* example of the Humanistic approach to. . . etc."

My head began to turn, until I saw the grade when I got the paper back. It wasn't a bad grade at all, but not exactly what his enthusiasm had led me to expect. Little did I know that in my absence, fashion-sensitive Academia had been swept off its feet by the deconstructive performance of Jacques Derrida. To most, the time-honored Humanistic approach smelled like great-granny's old petticoat stored away in a dark, damp and dusty attic.

I've since learned that on this side of the Pacific, generosity is not in short supply when it is used to make people feel proud of themselves. This is indeed a rather noble thing to do. Yet, much as caffeine, alcohol, or any other narcotic stimulant, constant use runs the risk of causing it to lose its potency until you have to increase the dosage to get a buzz at all. This may sound exaggerated, but I have found that words like "good" and "fine" (depending on how much warmth is injected into the utterance) have all but lost their power to induce an inkling of pride on the part of the recipient. Often times, you have to resort to words like "fantastic," "super" and yes, the superlatives, in order to see a happy smile bloom on the recipient's face.

Recently, one of my students was so disheartened by a "not bad!" comment from me that it took me quite a while to cheer her up again. I am wondering what is going to happen when "Super!" and "Fantastic!" in turn lose their high-producing potency.

In addition to deflation, there is another downside to such verbal generosity. You can earn all the superlatives in your evaluations for the last 10 or 20 years of service with the same employer. You could have been told that you're *the* most valuable employee, *the best* "man" for the job, etc., but you never know how you're really valued until you're passed over for promotion, tenure or, when one morning the boss summons you into his or her office, and hands you a pink slip. "Sorry, we'll have to let you go. . . " Condolences with no explanation.

Yet American civilization seems to thrive upon its ability to encourage people to feel proud. Come to think about it, what would have happened if a certain politically precocious boy named Bill from a small town called Hope of a small state called

Hubris and Humility: Is There a Happy Mean?

Arkansas if he had not been cheered all along by his single-parent mother when he was setting his sights on the Oval Office? We'd at least be having a much less ethical 42nd president. What if the parents of another young Bill, digitally precocious, had told him to get lost or dragged him to a psychiatrist when they found him daydreaming ("I am thinking here!") in their dimly-lit basement? To say the least, our drive on the information superhighway would be much bumpier.

All in all, though, an ability to feel proud and make others feel likewise signifies a culture's youth, vigor, confidence and boundless optimism. This is the gasoline fueling the engines of the *Mayflower* daring the storms of the Atlantic toward the New World, of boats braving the tempests of other waters toward Angel Island and Ellis Island, and of all the Apollos and Pathfinders venturing into outer space.

I was really being Chinese that morning when I responded miserably to the violin performance on the radio. Indeed, the Chinese tend to withhold praise, unless they are totally convinced, without a shadow of doubt, that what they are seeing is the real thing. They simply do not scream "Wow!" for you, excitedly, from the bottom of their hearts with their jaws hanging wide open at every opportunity.

In one of the best known scenes of the great 18th century Chinese novel, *Dream of the Red Chamber*, Jiazheng summons his teenage son Baoyu, before a group of honorable guests to test his poetic prowess. Touring the magnificent garden, the father would point at this flower or that fountain, and the son would have to compose a poem about it right then and there.

From all I know about poetry, Baoyu's sonnet-like poems measure up perfectly to the strict rules of versification, with all the proper rhyme, rhythm, and even some striking imagery. Every time, the father would dismiss the fruit of his son's creative labor, saying "Trash! Trash!" Poor Baoyu! No wonder he eventually lighted out for the mountains, and chose to live the reclusive life of a Taoist monk.

All children of Chinese descent living in this country can testify as to how hard it is to win a word of praise from their parents. One of the scariest days in their lives is when their report card is coming by mail. Even if they have always been straight-A students. They know too well that their parents' eyes will glide over all the perfect grades, only to be glued to any tiny imperfections. Their parents always like to see the bottle as at least one percent empty. They always expect more, and so do I. Tough love.

Most Chinese are not good on the receiving end of compliments, either. When you compliment a Chinese hostess on the wonderful food you've just enjoyed, more than likely the modest hostess would respond awkwardly, "Noooo, it's not good!" "Noooo, it's not tasty!" "Noooo, it's not delicious!"

Such rejection of compliment is usually instinctive and not affected at all. Yet it can be source of embarrassing cross-cultural misunderstandings. Remember the scene in *The Joy Luck Club* where a would-be American son-in-law takes such modesty from his would-be Chinese mother-in-law literally? It was Rich's first meeting with Waverly's mother, and in trying too hard to deliver a favorable impression, he violates every possible Chinese etiquette for table manners.

Worst of all, he takes his hostess's apologies ("This dish not salty enough. No flavor. Too bad to eat. Please. . . ") at face value, and takes it upon himself to correct the "problem" by pouring lots of soy sauce on an otherwise perfect fish dish. As Waverly bitterly comments, Rich has failed to take her mother's "insult" of her own favorite dish "as a cue to eat some and then proclaim it's the best she's ever made." What a mess! In this case, though, the hostess was actually fishing (pun intended) for compliments with her self-effacing comment.

Indeed, modesty has always been flaunted as a virtue in Chinese culture. From a very early age, a young Chinese mind is filled with such moral admonitions:

> *shan wai you shan, tian wai you tian,* There are greater mountains beyond mountains and there are higher skies beyond skies.
>
> *da zhi ruo yu,* A man of great wisdom often appears slow-witted.
>
> *san ren xing bi you wo shi,* Whenever three people travel together, at least one of them could be my teacher.
>
> *ren pa chu ming zhu pa zhuang,* Just as a pig is afraid of fattening, so should a human be afraid of acquiring fame.
>
> *shu da zhao feng,* The tallest tree in the woods gets thunderstruck first.

By the time he or she grows up, being modest has become second nature. That's probably why, having lived in this culture for almost 10 years, I am yet to cultivate the art of giving praises and taking compliments, earned or unearned, graciously.

Hubris and Humility: Is There a Happy Mean?

I used to wonder why the once-splendid Chinese civilization has somewhat faded during the last couple of centuries. But the answer seems obvious now. Absence of positive reinforcement for the last few millennia has finally traumatized her children, stunted their growth and creative power, and stifled their enterprising spirit to venture out into new territories.

So, if the Chinese are serious about reclaiming their lost glory, they've got to lighten up. They've got to stop being miserly with words and learn to say "Wonderful!" "Fantastic!" and "Super!" enthusiastically. Especially when it comes to their children.

"Gross oversimplification!" Some of my compatriots living in this country will say, utterly exasperated.

To avoid being accused of this crime, I will hasten to add that China has also had her share of pride and arrogance. In *The Journey to the West*, another great Chinese novel written in the 16th century, the protagonist, the Monkey King of a stone island on earth, was unhappy at being assigned the position of a mere stable boy in Heaven. To show his discontent, he not only helped himself to the forbidden Longevity Peaches in the royal orchard, but also wrought havoc in a Heaven presided over by the Jade Emperor, the god of gods. The punishment for his defiance was being buried alive under a five-peaked mountain for the next five thousand years.

Fiction aside, China looked upon herself as the center of the world up to the mid-1800s, hence her name in Chinese which means, "The Central Kingdom." This China-centric vision was not totally unfounded, of course. For quite a few centuries, Chinese civilization enjoyed a splendor largely unknown to civilizations in other parts of the world. Yet, geographically isolated at the far end of the Asian continent, she had never developed an interest in cross-civilizational intercourse, or the capacity for ocean voyages—despite the transcontinental "silk route"—to trade with other countries.

Being complacent, she disregarded anything outside the "center" as "barbaric." Of course, she paid dearly for her cockiness in the mid-1800s when her door was blasted open by "barbarians" with the gunpowder that she herself had invented. The wages of complacency were counted in tons of silver, stretches of land, thousands and perhaps millions of lives and deep humiliation.

More recently, in the 1950s, China bragged of having the largest population and thus the largest workforce in the world, and made plans accordingly to overtake England and U.S. within years that could be counted on fingers. She was punished for her big head, duly again, with disastrous tragedies.

Ironically, hubris has often been the hamartia, or tragic flaw, of a civilization that so celebrates humility as a virtue! This time around, however, China seems to have learned her lessons and found more or less a happy mean between hubris and humility. Given the current almost miraculous speed at which her economy is developing, her recently announced, ambitious plan to have accomplished complete modernization by the end of the 21st century so that she can feel proud again among the world civilizations is, to say the least, very modest.

Back to a personal note, the Fulbright professor could have been playing an innocent, semantic joke on three of his favorite students that summer in Beijing. Yet that joke may have prodded us to strive to be the best all these years. And who knows, given warm cheering along the way, that 12-year-old burgeoning violinist might blossom into another Paganini or Menuhin and receive an eager invitation to the Lincoln Center for the Arts.

Anything is possible.